METRICAL PIECES,

TRANSLATED AND ORIGINAL.

BY

N. L. FROTHINGHAM.

BOSTON:
CROSBY, NICHOLS, AND COMPANY,
111 WASHINGTON STREET.
1855.

CAMBRIDGE:
METCALF AND COMPANY, PRINTERS TO THE UNIVERSITY.

TO THE

FRIENDS OF MY LIFE,

AND OF

ITS LIGHTER STUDIES.

CONTENTS.

TRANSLATIONS.

FROM THE GREEK, LATIN, AND ITALIAN.

FROM THE GERMAN.

Schiller.

Herder.

Rückert.

ORIGINAL PIECES.

TRANSLATIONS.

THE PHENOMENA,

OR

APPEARANCES OF THE STARS.

TRANSLATED FROM THE GREEK

OF

ARATUS.

PREFACE.

THIS piece is at least a singular relic, if we are not permitted to call it a very poetical one, from the old world. It is singular for its unusual subject, its extreme simplicity of composition, and its extraordinary fortune. It was the first attempt, so far as we know, to represent in verse the groups and motions of the stars; and the design is carried through with a severe plainness, which may seem dry and insipid to modern taste. The poet appears to have relied for effect more upon the charm of his numbers than any ornaments of fancy. But though the work is thus technical in its matter, and unimaginative in its form, seeming to have little to invite popularity or even to preserve itself alive, — though the most eloquent of Roman scholars speaks of its author as not profoundly acquainted with the very phenomena he undertakes to describe,* and the most masterly of Roman critics dismisses him with the coldest of all praise, † — it has yet received marks of the highest favor in all ages, and arrived at distinctions such as few of the compositions of antiquity have reached. Ovid prophesied that it should live for ever with the luminaries it described. It was translated by Cicero, who, in questioning the science of the astronomer, expressed his admiration of the poet. It was translated again by Germanicus, the princely and beloved. After the mention of these names, one almost forgets the humbler one of Avienus, whose paraphrase appeared not less than four hundred years later. The magnificent poem of Manilius is under great obligations to it, and Virgil himself has frequently honored it with his use. Above all, the Apostle to the Gentiles has invested it with a sort of religious interest by quoting from it, with literal exactness, in his address to the Athenians at Mars' Hill: "For we are even His offspring." Doubtless, it was this high authority of St. Paul that introduced his

* Cicero, *De Oratore*, 1. 16.

† Quintilianus, 10. 1.

fellow-countryman — for Aratus also was a Cilician — to the Fathers of the Church. Their allusions to him, however, are short, and without any pretensions to criticism.

In later times he has been by no means neglected; as various editions of both his poems, the former of which only is here presented, abundantly testify. Hugo Grotius, before he was eighteen years old, devoted to it the first effort of his literary strength, as the great Roman orator had done before him. If Vossius could say, that it was wonderful how many Greek commentators had written upon it, whose works were lost, we may add that other annotations and comments have continued to be written, down to the present day, which may not perish so easily.

Yet, with all these claims on attention, the poem has never appeared in the English language. The translator offers this as an apology for the attempt he here makes to supply a literary deficiency. In performing his task, he has chosen to present the plain old bard literally, and in his own manner, rather than try to recommend him by modern airs and fancied embellishments. As for his poetical merits, which have been so variously judged of, we must at least concede something to the illustrious names that have reflected their praise upon him. And if we are compelled to say, with Delambre, that he was rather a versifier than either an accurate astronomer or a true poet, it yet will be but justice to add, with Bailly, that "time preserves only the works that defend themselves against it." *

The variations of the Greek text, and its discrepancies with the earliest versions, indicate that it has had its share of corruptions. The edition of Buhle, with its copious critical apparatus, seemed to leave nothing to be desired. But the present translation has availed itself, besides, of the later edition of Matthiæ; of that published in 1821 by the Abbé Halma, from manuscripts in the Royal Library at Paris; and of the readings of the learned Voss, — though with a prudent jealousy of his fondness for conjectural emendations.†

Boston, 1840.

---

* *Histoire de l'Astronomie Moderne,* I. 14.

† Two editions have been published since, one by Buttmann in 1826, and another by Bekker in 1828, both at Berlin; but these I have not seen.

POSTSCRIPT.

SINCE this Preface was written, and this translation completed, both the "Phenomena" and "Diosemeia" of Aratus have been rendered into English verse by Dr. John Lamb, Master of Corpus Christi College, Cambridge, and Dean of Bristol. This work was published in 1848. It is altogether too paraphrastic for fidelity; occasionally adding what is nowhere in the original, and omitting what it does not care to present. Its measure is sometimes defective and sometimes redundant, and its rhymes are frequently inadmissible. The name of the "Little Bear" it always writes "Cynosyra," in total disregard of the Greek diphthong, and in forgetfulness of many a beautiful line of English poetry; and, on the other hand, stars that have no names in the Greek text are spoken of under the Arabian titles, which were not bestowed upon them till centuries after the age of Aratus.

BOSTON, 1853.

THE APPEARANCES OF THE STARS.

FROM Jove begin we.* Let us never leave
Him uninvoked; for full of Jove are all
The paths of mortals; their assemblies all;
The sea is full, the harbors; — everywhere,
We all in all things need the aid of Jove.
FOR WE ARE EVEN HIS OFFSPRING.† Kind to men,
He shows good omens; spurs to toil the nations,
Reminding of life's needs; tells when the glebe
Is best for ox and spade; what hour 's propitious

---

* The Scholiast Theon says well at this place: "Very becomingly does Aratus, being about to declare the position of the stars, invoke in the beginning Jove, the Father and Maker of them. For by Jove is to be understood the Creator of the world."

† This is the passage quoted by St. Paul, Acts xvii. 28.

To set the plant and broadcast sow the seed.
For He in heaven these signs has firmly set,
Ordering the constellations; and each year
Appoints the stars to teach what man should do,
That all things may spring forth in their due season.
Him they propitiate, then, Him First and Last.*

Hail, Sire! all wonder, and all aid to men!
Hail, Thou and thy first offspring! hail, ye Muses,
Most gracious all! If rightly I invoke you
Singing the stars, inspire and fill the song.

Some fixed and many, others wandering wide,
Roll daily in heaven, continuous, without end;
Yet not a jot is moved the steady axis,

---

* Voss, in his translation, reduces the last words of this line to mere adverbs. And so the Scholiast understood them, who says: "This may refer to the libations; since the first of these was for the Olympian gods, the second for heroes, and the last for Jupiter the Saviour." But the text will bear perfectly well the present nobler interpretation.

Unalterable, but holds on all sides poised
The central earth, while round it sweeps the sky.
Two poles, one at each end, its limits mark,
One out of sight, one at the opposite North
High up from Ocean.
Close surrounding it
Two BEARS revolve *together*, — thence called *Wains*,* —
Which keep their heads for ever toward the haunches
Each of the other; back to back they move,

---

* The play upon words, in this mistaken etymology, cannot be represented in English, and is trifling enough in the Greek. The simple fact is, that the larger of these constellations was known by the different names of the *Bear*, and the *Wain* or *Ox-Cart*, as early as the time of Homer. This diversity in the image of so conspicuous a group of stars might have arisen from the opposite associations of the hunter's and the herdsman's life. "It is a curious coincidence, that among the Algonquins of the Atlantic and of the Mississippi, alike among the Narragansetts and the Illinois, the north star was called the *Bear*." — Bancroft's *History of the United States*, Vol. III. p. 314. Aulus Gellius has one of his pleasantest little narratives, Lib. II. cap. 21, about the Bear, Wagon, or, as the Romans called it, the Septemtriones.

By turns supine and upright. If we credit
The tale, from Crete by Jove's great favor these
Ascended into heaven. He was their nursling.
On fragrant Dictos, near the Idæan mount,*
They lodged him in a cave a year, and fed him;
While Saturn was deceived by the Dictæan
Curetes. One they name the Cynosura,†
The other Helice. The Grecian sailor
By Helice directs his bark; Phœnicians,

---

* There is not the least authority for the new reading of Voss in this passage; and the mythologists and geographers may be left to settle the difficulty of the text as they best can.

† The Great Bear, Boötes, and the Hound of Orion, are mentioned by Homer; Arcturus, and the Hound, by his name Sirius, are mentioned by Hesiod; and the Pleiades, the Hyades, and Orion, by both those ancient poets. The only constellations that are alluded to beyond doubt in the Holy Scriptures are the Dragon, the Pleiades, Orion, and the Bear. Amos v. 8; Job ix. 9, xxvi. 13, xxxviii. 31, 32. The "Arcturus" of Job, xxxviii. and ix., is now generally understood by the learned to be the Great Bear. — The Little Bear was introduced into Greece by Thales from the East, whence, indeed, came most of the other constellations, especially those of the Zodiac. We must admit this, notwithstanding the assertion of Pliny to the contrary, *Hist. Nat.* 2. 8.

Confiding in the former, plough the deep.*
Clearest, indeed, and readiest to the sight,
Shines broadly Helice at earliest eve;
But her small mate best guides the mariner,
Revolving in a narrower round than she
By her too the Sidonians voyage straightest.†

The twain disparting, like a river's flood,‡
Vast wonder, rolls the DRAGON, bending round
His coil immense; while upon each side stand
The Bears, safe lifted from the dark-blue sea.§

---

* "And thou shalt be our star of Arcady,
Or *Tyrian* Cynosure." — *Milton's Comus.*

† "Esse duas Arctos; quarum Cynosura petatur
Sidoniis, Helicen Graia carina notet."
Ovid. Fasti, 3. 107, 108.

‡ "Maximus hic flexu sinuoso elabitur Anguis
Circum, perque duas, in morem fluminis, Arctos."
Virg. Georg. 1. 244 - 246.

§ "Arctos, Oceani metuentes æquore tingi." — *Georg.* 1. 247.
"—— liquidique immunia ponti." — *Ovid. Fasti,* 4. 575.
"Οἴη δ' ἄμμορός ἐστι λοετρῶν 'Ωκεανοῖο."
Il. 18. 489, and *Odys.* 5. 273.

One with his tail he measures, stretching far,
While in his folds he clasps the other; its tip
Rests at the head of the bear Helice,
While Cynosura's head lies in that coil,
Which thence descending reaches to her foot,
And thence again twines backward. Nor from one
Point, nor with single star, his huge head shines:
Two in his temples beam, two in his eyes,
While one yet lower studs the monster's jaw.
That head aslant seems nodding towards the tail
Of Helice, with whose extremest end
The jaw and the right temple range in line.*
Itself keeps floating near about the spot,
Where furthest West and East embrace each other.

Near it there rolls, like to a struggling man,

* The objection of Hipparchus, that we should read "the *left* temple," was hasty. The image of the Dragon, according to Eudoxus, which is that described by Aratus, shows both temples; — presenting the front face and not the profile.

An IMAGE none knows certainly to name,*
Nor what he labors for. But yet they call him
Engonasin; † because upon his knees
Crouching he seems; while over both his shoulders
His hands are spread, on this side and on that,
A fathom wide; and full upon the forehead
He tramples with his foot the crooked Dragon.

There too that CROWN, which Bacchus set on high, ‡
A brilliant sign of the lost Ariadne,

---

* "Nixa venit Species genibus, sibi conscia causæ."
Manil. 1. 322.

† Engonasin; that is, the Kneeling One; so named, or rather forborne to be named, by Ptolemy. "Ignota facies," adds Manilius, 5. 646. It is remarkable that Aratus always speaks of this constellation as if with a superstitious reserve. See line 614. The name it now bears is Hercules. Dr. Lamb thinks "no one can doubt (?) that this figure represents our first parent Adam after the Fall."

‡ "Gnosia stella Coronæ." —*Virg. Georg.* 1. 222. "Coronam Gnosida." — *Ovid. Fasti*, 3. 457, 458.

Rolls 'neath the shoulder of the wearied Image.
His shoulder nears the Crown; but for his
head,
Seek it by that of OPHIUCHUS. Hence
You may point out that glittering SERPENT-BEARER
Himself. Below the head the shining shoulders
How manifest! e'en in the full moon's light
They may be seen. The hands indeed match not,
Where only here and there a thin ray glimmers.
Yet still not unobservable, nor mean,
E'en these; but they are burdened with the
Snake,
That girdles Ophiuchus. He, firm fixed,
With both his feet tramples that mighty beast,*
The Scorpion, on the eye and breastplate standing
Erect; while in both hands the Serpent writhes, —
Small in the right, but in the left reared high,
And ending with his maw close to the Crown.

---

* Our poet is here at fault. Only the left foot of Ophiuchus presses the Scorpion.

Under his coil seek for the mighty CLAWS;*
Though these are scant of beams, in nothing splendid.

Just behind Helice, moves like a driver
ARCTOPHYLAX, whom men BOÖTES call,†
Because he seems to urge the wain of the Bear; —
In each part shining, but beneath his zone
Outshines the rest ARCTURUS, radiant star.

Below Boötes' feet thou seest the VIRGIN,
An ear of corn held sparkling in her hand.

---

* The ancient name of the seventh sign of the Zodiac was *Claws* (Chelæ), that is, of the Scorpion. The substitution of Libra, the Balance, with its corresponding picture, has been ascribed by some to Julius Cæsar. See Virgil's *Georg.* 1. 32-35.

† This constellation is called either Arctophylax, *Bear-Keeper*, or Boötes, *Herdsman*, according as Helice is pictured as a Bear or a Cart. The poet confounds the two figures together in the next line. See note, p. 11.

> "The wind-shaked surge, with high and monstrous mane,
> Seems to cast water on the burning Bear,
> And quench *the guards* of the ever-fixed pole." — *Shakespeare.*

Whether the daughter of Astræus, who
First grouped the stars, they say, in days of old, —
Or whencesoever, — peaceful may she roll!
Another fable runs, that once on earth
She made abode, and deigned to dwell with mortals.
In those old times, never of men or dames
She shunned the converse; but sat with the rest,
Immortal as she was. They called her Justice.
Gathering the elders in the public forum,
Or in the open highway, earnestly
She chanted forth laws for the general weal.
Not yet was known contention mischievous,
Nor fierce recrimination, nor uproar.
So lived they. Far off rolled the surly sea.
No ship yet from a distance brought supplies,
But ploughs and oxen brought them. Queen of
nations,
Justice herself poured all just gifts on man.
As long as earth still nursed a golden race,
There walked she; — but consorted with the silver

Rarely, and with reserves, nor always ready;
Demanding the old customs back again.
Nor yet that silver race she quite forsook.
At evening twilight, from the echoing mountains
She came alone. No gracious words fell from her;
But when the people filled the heights around,
She threatened and rebuked their wickedness,
Refusing, though besought, to appear again:
" How have your golden fathers left a race
Degenerate! But you shall breed a worse.
And then shall wars, and then shall hateful blood-
shed,
Be among men; and grief press hard on crime."
This said, she sought the mountains; and the
people,
Whose eyes still strained upon her, left for ever.
And when these also died, those others sprang,
A brazen race, more wicked than the last.
These first the sword, that road-side malefactor,
Forged; these first fed upon the ploughing oxen;

And Justice then, hating that generation,
Flew heavenward, and inhabited that spot
Where now at night may still be seen the Virgin,
Near the far-seeing Driver. O'er her shoulders
[In the left wing, and called VINDEMIATOR] *
Revolves a star, in size and light as wondrous
As hangs upon the tail of the Great Bear.†
Glittering is she, — the Bear, — and bright the
stars
Near her; — thou needest none to guide thy gaze.
How large and beauteous that before her feet!
One 'neath the shoulder; one below the loins;
At the hinder knees another; ‡ — but they all
Without or name or figure separate roll.

---

* This line is found in the editions of Halma and Matthæi. It is rejected, however, by Buhle, and translated neither by Germanicus, Avienus, nor Voss.

† Undoubtedly Vindemiator, the Vintager, is here intended, though praised quite highly enough. "At non effugit Vindemitor," *Ovid. Fasti*, 3. 407, where is related the fable of its origin.

‡ Cor Caroli, the Hunting Dogs, and the Hair of Berenice are supposed to be here denoted. The whole passage, however, is

Under her head the TWINS appear, below
Her middle is the CRAB. Beneath her feet
The LION flames. There the sun's course runs
hottest.
Empty of grain the arid fields appear,
When first the sun into the Lion enters.
Then too the loud Etesian winds fall thick
On the broad sea. No time is this for oars
In voyaging. The wide ship then for me!
And let the helmsman stoutly brave the blast.

Wouldst thou discern the starry CHARIOTEER?
And has the fame come to thee of the Goat,
And of the Kids, who have so oft beheld
Men tost and driven on the darkening deep?

---

not a little perplexing. The description cannot be reconciled at all with our image of the Bear. Dr. Lamb has interpreted the three last stars "as those on the shoulder, loins, and knee of the Virgin" herself. An old Greek scholiast had understood it so before him. But what are we to think of "the hinder knees" of a lady? Delambre has truly said, that one would be very much puzzled to construct a celestial map, or globe, from the descriptions of Aratus. *Histoire de l'Astronomie Ancienne*, Vol. I. p. 74.

Thou 'lt find him, whole and large, left of the Twins
Inclining; while the head of Helice
Turns opposite. On his left shoulder rests
The sacred Goat, — said to have suckled Jove;
Olenian Goat of Jove the priests have named
her.*
She indeed large and splendid; but not so
The Kids, that glimmer faintly at his wrist.

Close by his feet see couch the hornèd BULL!
Fit signs attend him. How distinct his head!
There needs no other mark upon his front,
So do the stars on both sides figure it.
And oft their name is mentioned. Who hears not
Of the Hyades, sprinkling his forehead o'er?
The tip of his left horn, and the right foot
Of the near Charioteer, one star embraces.†

---

* "Nascitur Oleniæ signum pluviale Capellæ."
Ovid. Fasti, 5. 112.

† The present name of this star is El Nath.

Together they 're borne on; but aye the Bull
The earlier sets, though coupled thus he rises.

Nor shall the hapless race of Jasian CEPHEUS *
Remain unsung; for of these, too, the name
Has reached to heaven; since they were kin to Jove.

---

* It would be but waste of time to enter here upon any mythological details, which are very variously rehearsed. They may easily be found in the Classical Dictionaries by those who value such learning, or think the search worth their care. One word of protest, however, against an old whim that it has been lately proposed to revive. This whim desires nothing less than to dispossess all those fabulous personages of the places they have occupied so long, and change into Christian titles the whole nomenclature of the heavens. Julius Schiller, in 1627, urged such a revolution in his "Cœlum Stellatum Christianum." He had been preceded by Schickard, Bartsch, and others. According to these worthies, the Great Bear becomes the Skiff of St. Peter; Cassiopeia, Mary Magdalene; and Perseus with Medusa's Head, David with the head of Goliath. The Cross in the Swan is the Holy Cross; the Virgin is Mary; the Water-Pourer, John the Baptist. The Dog belongs to Tobit, and the Triangle represents the Trinity. Something had been attempted in the same direction, it would seem, even still earlier. According to Athanasius Kircher, the Christian Arabs gave to the stars in the square of the Great Bear the name of the Bier of Lazarus; the three in the tail being Martha, Mary, and the Maid. The name

Cepheus himself, just behind Cynosura,
Stands like one spreading both his arms abroad.
Equal the line, drawn from her tail's extreme
To his feet, with that which both feet separates.*

But from his zone look but aside a little,

Benetnasch, which the last of these three still holds, and which means in the Arabic *Daughters of the Bier*, seems to confirm this account. It was probably given at first to the whole of the row.

Another gentleman, named Weigel, was of quite a different taste, and appears to have thought that nothing was so beautiful as the blazonry of heraldic devices. He accordingly turned all the starry figures into the various escutcheons of the princes of Europe. Out of the stars in the Swan he fashions the Electoral Swords; out of those of the Eagle, Dolphin, and Antinous, the Prussian Eagle; out of those of the Charioteer, the Trefoil, the ensign of France. In the region where the constellation Orion glitters, he paints the Roman two-headed eagle. Napoleon once found his way into the heavens, though I forget to whom he owed this short-lived apotheosis. We are more likely to dispense altogether with picture shapes, as the Chinese are said to do, than to change those that have been handed down to us. As for names, when they are once fixed, they should not be trifled with. History and science have an interest and property in them.

* This does not correspond with the figure of Cepheus now; and Hipparchus complained of the inaccuracy in his day.

Just by the first coil of the crooked Drag-
on ;* —
There rolls unhappy, not conspicuous
When the full moon is shining, Cassiepeia.†
Not many are the stars, nor thickly set,
That, ranged in line, mark her whole figure out,
But like a key that forces back the bolts ‡
Which kept the double door secured within, —
So shaped, her stars you singly trace along.

---

* It is the second coil, according to the present configuration of the sphere.

† Hipparchus justly finds fault with the poet for representing Cassiope as no brighter. She certainly figures with distinguished splendor in the sky. — Lach, in a learned dissertation on the names of the stars, in Eichhorn's "Allgemeine Bibliothek," B. 7, mentions the "cathedra mollis" of Juvenal (*Sat.* 6. 91) among the titles of this "lady in the chair." The supposition is quite unfounded, to say the least of it. But it is not so ludicrous as the mistake ascribed to Bayer, of making Aben Ezra one of the names of Cassiope, — mistranslating Scaliger's words: "Sic etiam hebraice vocavit Cass. Aben Ezra."

‡ For the key-shape of this group of stars, the curious reader may consult Huetius's note on Manilius, 1. 361. The substance of it, with a diagram, is presented by Dr. Lamb.

O'er her thin shoulders while she lifts her hands,
Thou wouldst believe her grieving for her child.*

And there revolves herself, image of woe,
ANDROMEDA, beneath her mother shining.
I hardly think thou 'lt search the night long for her;
So bright her head, — so bright her shoulders both, —
Her feet's extremities, and all her vesture.
Yet there, e'en there, her arms are stretched and fastened.
In heaven itself are chains for her. For ever
Those hands must keep their posture and their bonds.

The huge HORSE o'er her head is driven on,†

---

* "That starred Ethiop queen, that strove
To set her beauty's praise above
The Sea-Nymphs, and their power offended." — *Milton.*

† "Suspice; Gorgonei colla videbis Equi.
Nunc fruitur cœlo, quod pennis ante petebat."
Ovid. Fasti, 3. 448, 455.

Drawn to his middle; with whose lowest point
And her head's crown, one star in common shines.*
With that three others, at the sides and shoulders,
Beauteous and wide, compose a perfect square.†
In no proportion to them is the head,
Or neck, though long. But yet the farthest star,
Fixed in the burning nostril,‡ might e'en vie
With those four brilliant ones that best define him.
He 's not four-footed; — with no hinder parts,
And shown but half, rises the sacred Horse.
They say that he to lofty Helicon
Brought the pure spring of copious Hippocrene.
For upon Helicon no streams flowed down,
Till the Horse smote it; then the abundant waters
Gushed at the stamp of his fore-hoof. The shepherds
First called it Hippocrené, — the Horse-Fountain.

---

* Now called *Alpheraz;* Arab. *The Horse.*

† "The Square of Pegasus."

‡ The star *Enif;* Arab. *Nose.*

Still from the rock it pours; not far from where
The Thespians dwell, thou seest it; — but the Horse
Circles in heaven, and there thou must behold him.

Near are the rapid courses of the Ram;
Who, though he runs the widest rounds of all,
No less keeps up with the Bear Cynosura.
Languid, indeed, and poorly starred, as when
One looks by moonlight; yet not far below
The girdle of Andromeda thou 'lt find him.
Midway he cleaves the broad expanse; even where
The Claws roll, and Orion's glittering belt.
And yet another sign thou shalt discover
Beneath Andromeda. Three lines compose
The Triangle; on two sides measured equal,
The third side less. It is not difficult
To be discerned, more luminous than many.
Southward of these not far, twinkles the Ram.

On further, in the portals of the South,
The FISHES shine; one higher than the other,
And closer heedful of the rushing North.
From each of them extends as 't were a band,
That fastens tail to tail, as wide it floats;
And one star, large and brilliant, clasps its ends, —
The Heavenly Knot 't is called.* The Northern Fish
By the left shoulder of Andromeda
Is fitly designate, lying so near it.

Her lover, PERSEUS, seek for by her feet,
Which ever at his shoulders are revolving.
Tallest of all his compeers at the North
He towers. His right hand stretches toward the chair
Of his bride's mother. Swift, like one pursuing,
Dusty he strides through Jove's parental heavens.†

---

* Now *El Rischa;* Arab. *The Cord.*

† The expression "dusty," or "raising a dust," is the Homeric

Near his left knee, together clustered, all
The PLEIADES move on.* To hold the whole
Needs no great space, and they are faint to sight.
As seven, their fame is on the tongues of men,†
Though six alone are beaming on the eye.
Not that a star has e'er been lost from heaven,
As from our youth we 've heard; absurdly so
'T was fabled. These the seven names they bear:
Alcyone, and Merope, Celæno,
Taÿgeta, and Steropé, Electra,
And queenly Maia. Small alike and faint,
But by the will of Jove illustrious all,
At morn and evening, since he makes them mark
Summer and winter, harvesting and seed-time.‡

---

way of describing great speed. The idea of some, that allusion is here made to the circumstance of one of the hero's feet being in the Milky Way, appears to me very far-fetched.

* The Pleiades, though now accounted a part of the constellation of the Bull, were spoken of and painted as separate from it by the ancient astronomers.

† "Quæ septem *dici*, sex tamen *esse* solent." — *Ovid. Fasti*, 4. 167.

‡ I follow here a conjectural emendation of Voss, as confirmed by the version of Avienus.

The SHELL, too, is but small, which Hermes
bored,*
Yet in his cradle, and bade name the LYRE.
He placed it by the inexplicable IMAGE
In lifting it to heaven. † The rigid shape
With his left knee approaches it; his head ‡

---

* Great injustice is here done to the Lyre, whose principal star is among the very finest in the sky.

† These three lines are obscure; and, though found in Hipparchus, are passed over by the Latin translators. Buhle says that they still want help. The present version makes use of a conjectural reading of Voss, which is yet not perfectly satisfactory. Hermann, on the contrary, finds no difficulty in the case. For "rigid," he would have "winged"; supposing the figure to be that of the Vulture, who was formerly represented as holding the Lyre in his claws. Such a figure is certainly of great antiquity. The Arabian name for the principal star in the Lyre, *Vega*, is generally supposed to denote the *falling* or *lighting* Vulture. Hermann is offended with Bode for omitting the Vulture in his picture of the Ptolemaic constellations. Ovid certainly speaks of the sign, in one instance, under the name of *Milvus*, the *Kite* (*Fasti*, 3. 793); but Krebs maintains, at the place, that no such constellation is mentioned by any writer on astronomy before the time of Ovid.

‡ "His head" is far from being so situated; and this seems to me the chief difficulty.

Just opposite the Bird. The Lyre itself
Between that knee and the Bird's head is stationed.

In heaven, too, flies the variegated BIRD,*
Himself but dim, though still his pinions roughen
With stars not large, that shed a moderate light.
He thus, as one that floats on well-poised wings,
Propitious seeks the West; — at the right hand
Of Cepheus his right talons stretching forth,
While his left wing brushes the Horse's hoof.

Him as he springs the Fishes twain attend;
While by that Horse's head the WATER-POURER
Spreads his right hand, just behind CAPRICORN.†
Before him, further westward, lies inclined
That GOAT himself, where the Sun's might turns
back.

---

* This "Bird" was called the "Swan," as far back as Eratosthenes. We must acknowledge that our poet gives but a poor account of this beautiful constellation.

† "Jam levis obliquâ subsedit Aquarius urnâ."

Ovid. Fasti, 2. 456.

Not in this month surround thee with the sea,
Crossing its broad expanse. For little progress
Thou 'lt make by day, since now the days run
shortest;
Nor, as thou tremblest at the night, will dawn
Hasten to meet thee, call thou ne'er so loud.
Then blow the fearful south-winds, when the
Goat
With the sun rises; and then Jove's sharp cold,
Still worse, besets the stiffening mariner.
But ah! the whole year through, beneath the
keels
The sea will darken; — while, like water-fowl,
Oft gazing from the ships across the deep,
We sit with eyes tow'rd shore. That shore far off
Is wave-beat; — one small plank 'twixt us and
Hades.*

* Much has been said of the beauty of this passage, in which the poet seems to have had in mind a line of the Iliad, 15. 628. Longinus, however, chooses to criticise it (§ 10), as being too minute to be sublime, — a judgment in which many will dissent from him.

Thou, who the former month hast sailed distressed,
When the Sun kindles up the Bow and Archer,
Seek evening ports, nor longer trust the night.
A signal of that season and that month
The SCORPION be, rising as night departs.
For, closely towards his sting, his mighty bow
The ARCHER draws. A little in advance
Comes into sight the Scorpion; he hard after.
Then Cynosura's head in the sinking night
Mounts high; and, ere the morning dawns, down go
Crowded Orion, and from hand to loins
Cepheus.

There 's further shot another ARROW;
But this without a bow. Towards it the BIRD
More northward flies; while near it soars a second,
Smaller in size, but stormy from the sea
Rushing, as night returns. He 's named the EAGLE.*

* "Tunc oritur magni præpes adunca Jovis." — *Ovid. Fasti*, 6. 195.

The Dolphin, small to sight, floats o'er the Goat,
Dim in the midst, but four fair stars surround him;
One pair set close, the other wider parted.
Between the North and the sun's winding way
Are these diffused. Afar off, many others,
Between that solar path and the South, ascend.

Aslant, below the section of the Bull,
Orion's self! What eye can pass him over,
Spreading aloft in the clear night? Him first *
Whoever scans the heavens is sure to trace.

Then what a sentinel beneath his feet,
As high he rears his back, the Dog appears!
Various he shines, not all illuminated;
The body faintly sparkling, but the chin
Glows with a brilliant star, that scorches sharply,
And hence men call it Sirius.† All the gardens

---

* "Armatumque auro *circumspicit* Oriona." — *Virg. Æn.* 3. 517.

† The word "Sirius" is applied to the Sun as well as to the Dog-

Mistake it not, their green leaves drained of
moisture,
When with the sun it rises. Piercing deep,
It tries their planted rows; some trees it hardens,
While from the rest the guardian bark it strips.
When it sets, too, we hear of it; the stars
That trace the limbs twinkling more feebly round.

Under Orion's feet mark too the HARE,
Perpetually pursued. Behind him Sirius
Drives as in chase, — hard pressing when he rises,
And when he sinks as hotly pressing still.

---

star by the ancient Greek poets whose works are still extant; and, if we may trust to Hesychius, was used of all the stars by the poet Ibycus, whose death is said to have been avenged by the cranes upon his murderers, but his verses have not been spared by time. Claudian, too, speaks of the "Siria sidera," *Laud. Hero.* 124.

No star has been so signalized by poetry as this brightest one in the heavens. Our poet, in his other poem, calls it the Κύνα θρασὺν Ὠρίωνος (*Arat. Diosem.* 23). Some represent it as *barking fire*: "Latratque Canicula flammas." — *Manil.* 5. 526. "Nec gravidis allatret Sirius uvis." — *Claud. De Laud. Stil.* 466. Achilles in arms pursuing Hector is compared by Homer to its brilliant but baleful light. (*Il.* 22. 30.)

Against the tail of the great Dog is dragged
Sternward the ARGO, with no usual course,
But motion contrary; —'as ships themselves,
When they who steer them turn their beaks
about,
Entering the port. Each sailor presses aft
The vessel then, that backward meets the shore.
So sternward labors the Jasonian Argo; —
Obscure in parts and starless, as from prow
To mast; but other portions blaze with light.
Below the hind feet of the Dog, who hastens
Still forward constantly, the rudder swings.

Though hovering far aloft, Andromeda
Is threatened by the onset of the WHALE.
She by the breath of Thracian Boreas
Is swept inclined; while the south wind drives
on
That Whale, her foe, beneath the Ram and Fishes,
And just above the starry RIVER, placed.

For O how flows beneath the feet of the gods*
The remnant of Eridanus,† — that stream
Tear-sprinkled, which Orion's left foot laves!
The Bands, that hold the Fishes twain together,
And downwards float from each extremity,
Behind the Whale's back gather into one,
And in one star they terminate, that rests
On the first prickle of the monster's spine.‡

Of small dimensions, and of feeble ray,
Between the Whale and Rudder circle stars,
Hovering below the Hare's resplendent sides,
Without a name. For to no shapely figure

---

* "Me nocte premunt vestigia Divûm," sings Catullus, in the person of Berenice's Hair: 66. 69.

† "The *remnant* of Eridanus" seems to refer to the shrunken state of that river, the Po, under the misadventure of Phaëton, whose death and the sorrows of his sisters are implied in the following line. Hermann thinks that the phrase may also allude to the small part of this constellation that rises into view in the Northern hemisphere. But the poet had not probably two meanings.

‡ See p. 29.

Their scattered host bears likeness; as do many,
That grouped in order follow the same paths
Of circling years. Some man of ages past
Observed their goings; and devised their titles,
Forming the constellations. For the name
Of each star singly none could tell or learn; —
So numerous are they everywhere, and many
Of the same size and color, as they roll.
Thus he bethought him to combine them so,
That, ranged in neighborhood, they might present
Images,* — each taking his proper name,

---

* I cannot refrain from translating here an animated passage from the distinguished German writer on astronomy, Schubert: — "To the astronomer the fixed stars are immovable boundary-stones, by which he determines the courses of the wandering heavenly bodies. To the geographer they are the signal-stations, according to which he surveys the chart of the earth at the heavens. To the mariner they are the lights that direct him over the dark paths of the seas. To the hunter, the herdsman, the wanderer, they are a clock. To the farmer, they are a calendar. The historian finds in them many a memorable event in the oldest Grecian history; the poet, the charming Grecian mythology, which has furnished such rich materials to dramatic art; and every person of sensibility, an impulse to worship, meditation, and hope."

And henceforth none rising to doubt or guess at.
These, in clear figures gathered, meet the sight;
But those that hang beneath the hunted Hare
All indistinct and nameless go their way.

Underneath Capricorn and Southern breezes,
Turned towards the Whale there swims a FISH
aloft,
Of the other pair sole progeny,* and named

* Duncan in his "Religions of Profane Antiquity," says that the Zodiacal Fishes were supposed to be the progeny of the Piscis Australis; — rather unnaturally, and I know not on what authority. I have here followed, with some hesitation, the version of Hermann, in his "Handbuch der Mythologie," 3 Theil. Voss and Halma understand the words as alluding only to the solitary position of the Fish. This is the star *Fomalhaut*. The name is from the Arabic, whence a great part of the present titles of the stars are borrowed, and means *The Mouth of the Fish*. It is therefore not to be pronounced *Fomalo,* as a very respectable work on Astrognosy has directed. I refer to Burritt's "Geography of the Heavens," a valuble elementary book, excelling perhaps every other of its kind in the copious information that it gives, on points where the young student most needs it. But it has several blemishes of this kind, indicating here and there a defective learning. Thus, it speaks of the principal star in the constellation of the Lion as named Regu-

The SOUTHERN one. More scattered stars, below
The Water-Pourer, and between the Fish
And skyey Whale, mount dull and undistinguished.
But on the splendid Water-Pourer's right,
And near those last, — as 't were a little gush
Of water, scattered sparkling to and fro, —
Others of loveliest aspect modest roll.
Among them two, nor close nor widely parted,
Shed more conspicuous beams; one bright and broad
At the Water-Pourer's feet, the other set
In the azure monster's tail. These all alike
The name of Water share. A few — they small —

---

lus, "from the illustrious Roman consul of that name." Whereas the word is the diminutive of Rex, and means Prince. It was first given to it, according to Ideler ("Untersuchung über den Ursprung und die Bedeutung der Sternnamen"), by Copernicus. There are great faults of taste also in the performance. But for real use it far exceeds some popular treatises from abroad, that are remarkable chiefly for their vague sentimentality, their visionary speculations, and their false brilliants.

Beneath the Archer's forward feet revolve,
Bent round into the semblance of a crown.*

Under the burning sting of that huge beast,
The Scorpion, near the South the ALTAR rises.
Look quick, for but short time wilt thou behold it.†
Over against Arcturus it is reared,
Of which full loftily the circuits run,
While this sinks quick beneath the Western sea.
Yet in this Altar has primeval Night,‡

---

* If the reading that is here followed be the true one, the Southern Crown is plainly indicated. But objection has been made, that this figure is not to be found in any table of the stars at so early a period. Voss adopts a conjectural reading from Grotius, and gives a different turn to the passage.

† The constellation of the Altar does not rise into our latitude.

‡ According to the Grecian mythology, Night was the original Mother; having produced both the gods and men.

"Νύκτα θεῶν γενέτειραν, ἀείσομαι, ἠδὲ καὶ ἀνδρῶν." — *Orphic.*

"To say that Night was senior to Day, implied that the world had a beginning," says Cudworth, after quoting the above passage.

"Night, *All-Mother of life*, I praise thee, glorious goddess,
Queen! there is none like thee, that crowneth her head with stars."
Friedrich Rückert.

Pitying the weary lot of mortals, placed
A great sea-sign of storms. For near her heart
Lay the imperilled ships ; — and elsewhere other
Signals she shows, pitying the tempest-tost.
Pray not that, as I voyage all-o'erclouded,
This constellation may shine out in heaven,
Cloudless itself and lustrous. Rather loaded
With billowy darkness be it ; such as presses
Frequent and thick when Autumn winds arise.
For oft this sign gives in the South old Night,
In kindness to hard-faring mariners.
Let them give heed, when she 's propitious thus ; —
Easy and smooth then all at once becomes,
And their whole task is light. But should the tempest
Strike from above with its fierce blast the ship,
Quite unforeseen, and shatter every sail,
Then are they hurried down beneath the surges ;
Or else by prayers they stay the passing Jove,
And the wind's might now from the North prevails.

Through thousand toils, again they see each other
On the firm deck. Dread thou, beneath this sign,
The South, till Boreas clears the turbid air.
But if from Western wave the Centaur's shoulder
Is far as from the Eastern, and a mist
Shrouds him a little, — while like token Night
Shows o'er the flaming Altar, — fear not then
The South so much, but dread the Eastern blast.

The CENTAUR seek beneath two other groups;
The human parts below the Scorpion lying,
Those of the horse held subject by the Claws.
He looks like one with right arm ever stretched
Towards the round Altar, and holds tight in hand
Some beast that he had hunted.* So at least
The former ages hand it down to us.

But lo! afar another constellation!
They call it HYDRA. Like a living creature,

* This hunted animal is the *Wolf*.

'T is long drawn out. His head moves on below
The midst of the Crab; his length below the Lion;
His tail hangs o'er the Centaur's self. Midway
His volume is the CUP *; and as he ends,
The figure of a CROW seems pecking at him.
See PROCYON, too, glittering beneath the Twins.

These mayst thou view, as the years hasten by,
Renew their hours in order; their fixed shapes
Are graven on the night-sky, never varied.
Five other stars, unsteady, always changing,†
Traverse on every hand those figures twelve.
From gazing at the rest, thou 'lt ne'er conjecture
Where these are placed, — such wanderers are
they all.

---

* "Crater auratis surgit cælatus ab astris."

Manil. 5. 235.

The story that is meant to account for the union of these three figures is told by Ovid, in his *Fasti*, 2. 243 - 266.

† Nothing seems wanting to the completeness of this description of the planets, as distinguished from the fixed stars, but the circumstance of their steady, untwinkling light.

Years upon years must mark their courses out,
And the slow signs look long ere they come
back.
More here I dare not; failing else to show
Of those fixed ones the circles and the signs.

Four circles,* rounded as by nicest art,
There are; — which they most wish and need to
know,
That track the measures of the travelling years.
About them all are plainly-lying signs
Many, in neighboring order well disposed; —

---

* These four circles are the Equator, the Ecliptic, and the two Tropics of Cancer and Capricorn. They are not drawn, as the student will perceive, with the accuracy of our modern globes and maps. How, indeed, could they be? Or how can we expect of a poet what was not made out by the deepest science of that age? Even M. Delambre, however, admits that, with a few modifications, and those of no great consequence, the constellations of Aratus are in the places where they truly belong. The Milky Way is here evidently regarded as one of the great circles of the sphere. It seems to be called "broad" to distinguish it from those lines "without breadth," which are yet not treated as if they were merely ideal.

They without breadth, all fitted to each other,
And their lines corresponding, two to two.

When haply in clear skies the heavenly Night
Reveals to men the concourse of bright stars,
Not one enfeebled by the full moon's light,
But from the darkness all flash sharply forth,
If then a sacred wonder fill thy mind,
Observing how the heaven is cleft throughout
By a broad circle, or should some one near thee
Point out that radiant belt, its name is MILK.
For colored so revolves no other circle;
Though in extent two of those four may match it,
The other two rolling in smaller rounds.

The first of these to the down-rushing North
Is neighbor; in it both Twins' heads are borne,
The knees of the well-fitted Charioteer,*

* The phrase "well-fitted" is supposed by the old scholiast to allude to the junction with the horn of the Bull. But this is not the most likely interpretation.

And the left leg of Perseus and the shoulder,
Then holds its way direct through the right side
Above the elbows of Andromeda;
Whose outstretched palm lies nearest to the North,
While to the South that bended elbow leans.
The hoofs next of the Horse, and of the Bird
The neck with the head's tip, and the fair shoulders
Of Ophiuchus, in that circle whirl.
A little further to the South the Virgin
Avoids it; but the Lion and the Crab,
These both it strikes, as they lie ranged together.
It cuts the Lion through the breast and body;
The other traversing the whole shell under,
Where thou perceiv'st him just in twain disparted,
So that each side of the line his eyes are set.
Into eight parts the whole distributed,
Five roll in day, o'er the Earth's upper parts;
Three in the lower. Here are Summer's turnings,
As round the Crab the Northern ring is fastened.

The other, in the opposite South, divides
The Goat, the Water-Pourer's feet, and tail
Of the Sea-Monster. In it lies the Hare,
But of the Dog little the feet except.
Argo is here, the Centaur's shoulder-blades,
The Scorpion's sting, the Archer's glittering bow;
Whom last, the sun, from the clear North descending,
Crosses, then wheels to the South, and wintry grows.
Of its eight parts but three revolve aloft,
While five pursue their subterranean way.

Midway twixt both, large as the Milky Way,
A halving circle undergirds the Earth.
Here days and nights are equal, each to each,
Of fading Summer and advancing Spring.
Its sign the Ram and the Bull's knees denote; —
The Ram's full length, the Bull's but bending joints.

Splendid Orion's belt it holds; the flexure
Of burning Hydra; the thin Cup; the Crow.
Stars, though not many, of the Claws it crosses,
And knees of the Serpent-Bearer. The swift Eagle
It intercepts not; but close by it storms
Jove's mighty Messenger. Near, too, the Horse
Carries his head and neck. All these the axis
Drives straight about, keeping the midmost place.

'Twixt the first two, the fourth is wedged obliquely.
The tropics on each opposite side retain it,
The midmost intersects it in the midst.
Though by Athene taught, no man would skill
To fasten otherwise the rolling wheels,
Such and so many spinning them around,
Like those well-fitted orbits in the heaven,
That every day from dawn to dark hold on.*

* There is no inconsiderable poetic grace in thus intimating the unhalting motion, day as well as night, of the stars.

And these are rising, those are going down,
Keeping their distance all. Of each in order,
Each side, the same departure and return.
But this by as much of Ocean's flood will vary
As lies between the ascending Goat and Crab;
The sinuous line will sink the space it rises.
Such length as the eye tracks, gazing to heaven,
This, six times told, it runs; each part drawn even
Cuts off two constellations.* And they call it

---

* This dark saying is at once made clear, if we reflect that the ancient astronomy, for the most part, supposed the earth's sphere to be suspended in the middle of space, equally distant at every point from the circle in which the heavenly bodies revolved around it. Of course, any line drawn, as the poet directs, to any point aloft, would be a radius, or semi-diameter, or sixth part, of the whole round; and this hexagon, if completed, would have two of the twelve constellations on each side. See Cicero's Tusculan Disputations, 5. 24. The same thing is expressed by Manilius, I. 544 – 552, where, in any good edition, may be found a diagram illustrating it. — I cannot avoid alluding, in this connection, to a very remarkable passage in Manilius, I. 168 – 170, in which the poet describes the earth as thus held in its place by opposite forces. "Therefore it remains firm," he says, "because the whole heaven flies from it just so far, and has made it to fall every way, that it might not fall." If, instead of "every way," we could read "al-

The Belt of Living Creatures, — Zodiac.
Here is the Crab, the Lion next, and 'neath him
The Virgin; here the Claws too, and the Scorpion,
The Archer, and the Goat, and close by him
The Water-Pourer. Here the Fish-Pair sparkle;
And after them the Ram, the Bull, the Twins.
Through all these twelve moves on the sun, completing
Each several year; and, as he moves his round,
There grow about his path the fruitful hours.

---

ways," there would nowhere exist so terse an account of the Newtonian theory of gravitation: —

"fecitque cadendo
Ne caderet."

For a beautiful description of the balancing of the round earth in space, see the Fasti of Ovid, Lib. 6, l. 267 – 278. In this description he makes mention of the glass sphere, the work of Archimedes, in which the motions of the heavenly bodies were represented. Such an Orrery — if one may venture the anachronism — is spoken of by Cicero in his Tusculan Questions, l. 25; and a fine epigram of Claudian, the 67th, is devoted to it. A high idea of this planetarium is suggested by the lines: —

"Percurrit proprium mentitus signifer annum,
Et simulata novo Cynthia mense redit."

Far as it dips below the hollow ocean,
So far it sweeps o'er earth; while every night
Six parts go down of its twelve-signed circle,
As many rise. So long spreads out each night
As this half-circle lifts of its degrees
Above the earth after the dark sets in.

Nor should he scorn, who watches for the day,
To mark when each of its portions shall ascend;
For aye with one of them comes up the sun
Himself; and thou mayst note them as thou
gazest.
But since or black with clouds or hid by moun-
tains
They sometimes rise, seek others bright to guide
thee.
These the great sea, from East and Western horn,
May grant to thee; since many such surround
him,
As from below each starry form he rears.

When the Crab rises, stars of no mean power
Lie on each side; some falling, some just risen.
Down goes the Crown; down to the spine the Fish.
Half of that vanishing Crown thou seest aloft,
The lowest half already gone;—but He
Of the form reversed his body scarcely shows,
Since all the upper parts revolve in night.
The laboring Ophiuchus, too, from knees
To shoulders, and his Snake e'en to the neck,
The Crab draws down. Nor of Arctophylax
Is much on either hand; of the day-part least;
The nightly portion has the advantage now.
Boötes sets through four of the signs,* before
Ocean receives him. When he 's lighted full,
What time the steer 's unyoked, he more than half
The night remains, though sinking with the sunset.

---

* Boötes begins to set with the rising of the Bull, sinks lower with that of the Twins and the Crab, and disappears at the coming up of the Lion.

Nights thus are marked by his slow-falling stars.*
So they go down. But on the opposite side,
In nothing mean, glittering in belt and shoulders,
And trusting in the might of his good sword,†
Bringing the whole STREAM ‡ with him, mounts
Orion.

Pressed by the rising Lion, all go down
That at the Crab retired; with them the Eagle;
And of the Kneeling One the knee alone
And left foot keep above the billowy sea.
Rise with him Hydra's head, the bright-eyed Hare,
And Procyon, and the burning Dog's fore feet.

---

* "'Οψὲ δύοντα Βοώτην," *Hom. Odyss.* 5. 272. "Piger ille Boötes," *Ovid. Fasti,* 3. 405. "Frigidæ circumagunt pigri sarraca Boötæ." *Juv.* 5. 23.

† "Ensiferi nimium fulget latus Orionis?" *Lucan. Phars.* l. 665.
"Et tribus obliquis demissus ducitur ensis." *Manil.* l. 398.
"Ensiger Orion." *Ovid. Fasti,* 4. 388.

‡ "Stelliger Eridanus sinuatis flexibus errans
Clara Noti convexa rigat, gladioque tremendum
Gurgite sidereo subterluit Oriona."
Claud. Cons. Honor. 176 – 178.

Nor few the stars that 'neath earth's lowest
parts
The rising Virgin drives. The Lyre Cyllenian,
And Dolphin, and the well-shaped Arrow, sink.
With them the Bird's wing-tip, close to the tail,
And the River's furthest bend are hid in shadow.
The Horse's head, the Horse's neck, descend.
Now Hydra rises to the very Cup.
The Dog, at length, uplifting his hind feet,
Draws after him the prow of starry Argo,
Who sails half-mast above the earth, what time
The Virgin's perfect image quits the deep.

Nor let the Claws, though faintly beaming, pass
Unnoticed when they rise. For great Boötes,
Gemmed with Arcturus, lifts his crowded form.
Argo will not be wholly up; but Hydra
Draws through the heaven his sinuous length,
save only
The ending point. The Claws lead on no more

Than from the right knee down of Him that
kneels
Always, and always stretches towards the Lyre;
Whose shape, mysterious 'mong its heavenly
mates,
Oft the same night is seen to go and come.
With the two Claws the leg alone ascends.
But He, with head reversed, awaits the Scorpion
Now rising, and the Archer; for these bring him;
The Scorpion to the middle; all the rest,
With the left hand and head, the Bow drives on.
Thus he, in three parts, through three signs re-
volves.
The Claws still rising carry half the Crown,
And the last waving of the Centaur's tail.
Down plunges then the Horse, whose head before
Had disappeared; and the preceding Bird
Drops her last feather from the upper sky.
The head, too, of Andromeda descends;
While the thick South impels the huge Sea-
Monster

Against her, and opposing from the North
Cepheus his great hand brandishes; the Whale
Settles to his back's ridge, but Cepheus only
In head and hand and shoulder falls from sight.

The windings of the River seek the embrace
Of the broad ocean, as the Scorpion comes,
Who with his coming frights e'en vast Orion.
O, be appeased, chaste Artemis! Not mine
The story, but from former days it comes,
That, when in Chios all the wild beasts fell
Beneath the strong Orion's massy club,
When at Œnopion's hest he played the hunter,
He dared profane her robes. From that same island,
Bursting the hills apart, another beast,
The Scorpion, she aroused; who bit and slew
The mighty one, — mightier than he himself
Through Artemis insulted. Hence, they say,
Soon as the Scorpion from his depth emerges,
Orion flies to hide him underground.

Nor of Andromeda, nor of the Whale,
The parts were dim that met his rising. Now
In haste they fly. Then with his girdle Cepheus
Grazes the earth, the parts about his head
Bathing in Ocean; all the rest prevented, —
The Bears refusing any leave to set.*
And she herself, the wretched Cassiepeia,
Still presses towards the image of her child.
Not from the chair her feet and hands are lifted
With quiet grace, but like a diver headlong
She plunges to the knees, — so not unpunished,
For rivalling fair Panope and Doris.
Thus westward borne she floats. But the eastern heaven
Rolls others up; the Crown's remaining round,†

---

* The Bears are here put for the Arctic Circle.

† "The Crown's remaining round." *Δεύτερα κύκλα* was supposed to denote the Southern Crown, by Hyginus and Scaliger. But this constellation, it is said, was not grouped till after the time of Hipparchus. With Voss, I follow Cicero and Avienus, the ancient translators. See page 54, lines 4 and 5, and the note on page 42, line 2.

The last of Hydra, with the Centaur's head
And body, and the creature he holds grasped
In his right hand. The Monster-Horseman waits,
With his fore feet, the rising of the Bow.

With the Bow rises Ophiuchus' form,
And the Snake's coil. The dreadful Scorpion brings
The heads of both, with the hands of Ophiuchus,
And the first glitter of the starry Serpent.
Lo, too, the Kneeling One! always reversed
He comes; and now his limbs and belt and bosom,
His shoulders and left hand, displays; the right one,
And head, will with the Bow and Archer rise.
With these the Hermean lyre, and to the breast
Cepheus, are starting from the Eastern wave.
Then all the splendors of the mighty Dog
Go down; Orion wholly; and the whole
Of the hunted Hare, whose chase is never done.
But not the Kids, nor the Olenian Goat,

Have sunk as yet; from the Charioteer's huge hand
They flash, from all his other limbs apart,
Waking the storms when with the sun they join.

But these at length — the head, the other hand,
And loins — ascending Capricorn thrusts down.
The lower stars all yield before the Archer.
E'en Perseus now resists not, nor the beak
Of starry Argo. But the hero sinks
To the knee and the right foot; her rounded poop
The vessel dips, as Capricorn comes up.
Then Procyon vanishes; but other groups,
The Bird, the Eagle, and the flying Arrow,
Rise, with the Southern Altar's sacred seat.

When half his form the Water-Pourer lifts,
The Horse rears head and hoofs; while, opposite,
The Centaur's tail sweeps from the starry night,

Which cannot yet his head and massy shoulders
And breast draw down, but of the fiery Hydra
The crooked neck and forehead full submerges.

Much of her still is left; but all, thick-studded,
Sinks with the Centaur, when the Fishes rise.
With these comes on the Fish,* that hangs below
The dusky Capricorn; but not yet wholly,
Waiting awhile till the next Twelfth appears.
So, too, the wretched hands, the knees and shoulders,
Of halved Andromeda, throughout disparted,
Rise when the Fishes twain emerge from Ocean.
The right-hand parts these bring; the left uplifts
The coming Ram, who, as he comes, reveals
From the far West the Altar. In the East
His head and shoulders lifts the rising Perseus.
Whether his zone shines with the ending Ram,
Or with the Bull, o'er whom he closely rolls,
Is doubtful. Now the rising Bull forsakes not

* "The Fish" is the Southern fish, Fomalhaut. See pp. 40, 41.

The Charioteer, who 's ever bound to him,*
Though not ascending wholly with that sign;
The Twins bring his full figure. But the Kids,
The sole of the left foot, the Goat herself,
Come with the Bull, when the long back and tail
Of the ethereal Whale rise from beneath.
Sinks now Arctophylax with that first sign,
Four of which draw him down,† save the left
hand
Still elevate, with the Great Bear revolving.‡

---

* Bound to him by the star El Nath, which is common to them both. See p. 22, note.

† See p. 54.

‡ I follow here the reading of Grotius's MS. which is adopted by Voss.

The familiar lines of Anacreon can scarcely fail to be here brought to the mind of the classical reader: —

Στρέφεται ὅτ' Ἄρκτος ἤδη
Κατὰ χεῖρα τὴν Βοώτου.

No English version of these lines, that I have ever seen, has presented the astronomical image that was in the mind of the poet. And yet it was of the more importance to present it, as it is there for its own sake. The turning of the Bear at the hand of Boötes does not designate the midnight hour above any other hour of the night. It is only a sparkling picture of the Night itself. The pic-

When both legs of descending Ophiuchus
Up to the knees are plunged, be sure the Twins
From the other side are coming. Then no part
Of the vast Whale is mounting or depressed,
But all in heaven you see him float abroad.
And now the sailor in the sea's clear glass
May see the RIVER's bend from ocean rising,
Waiting Orion's self; whether announcing
The measure of the night, or of the voyage; —
For everywhere the gods tell much to men.*

---

ture, therefore, as there was nothing but its own beauty to justify its introduction, should have been carefully preserved in translating.

* Voss supposes that this concluding line indicates the transition point from the "Phenomena" to the "Prognostics," another poem which is found immediately connected with the former in some manuscripts. On such a supposition, the line would resemble the star El Nath, that joins the tip of one of the horns of the Bull with the heel of the Charioteer; or El Rischa, that fastens the Band of the Fishes to the neck of the Whale. There may be some plausible ground for such an idea. The two pieces, however, are sufficiently distinct from each other. They have come down to us under separate titles; being borrowed, as is supposed, from two small works of Eudoxus, the Phenomena, and the Mirror, that were written not far from a hundred years before.

THE SHADE OF CORNELIA TO PAULUS.

PROPERTIUS, BOOK IV. ELEGY XI.

This closing Elegy of Propertius, a writer of the Augustan age, is a Héroide from the dead. The version is quite literal, and line for line. It gives an opportunity of comparing some of the purest sentiments of classical antiquity, respecting the state of the dead, with those of the simplest minds that have had the advantage of a Christian education. This Elegy has often been called " the queen of Elegies " ; and it deserves the title, which has thus, as by the common consent of scholars, been awarded to it. As an expression of those domestic affections which belong to no time, or country, or institutions, but to the common heart of man, it takes rank above everything of a like kind among the poets of that cultivated period. I know of nothing, within the same compass, that approaches it, as a picture at once of Roman pride, Roman opinion, and Roman manners.

CORNELIA TO PAULUS.

Cease, Paulus, with thy tears my tomb to pain ; *
The black gate opens to no prayer. 'T is vain.

---

* The ancients supposed that the dead were troubled by the immoderate grief of their friends.

When once we 've passed beneath death's lower
sway,
Relentless adamant bars up the way.
Though Dis should hear thee from his dusky halls,
The silent shores would drink each tear that falls.
Vows move Celestials. When the boatman 's paid,
The dismal door shuts in the parted shade.

So sang the funeral trumpets, when my head
Found, o'er the funeral torch, the pyre its bed.
What profit to be Paulus' wife? to claim
Ancestral cars, and living heirs of fame?
Would Fate for these extend Cornelia's days?
Lo, I 'm a weight that five small fingers raise! *

Detested glooms, thou grim flood's sluggish sheet,
Ye weedy waves that tangle round my feet!
Too soon, but guiltless, hither have I come;

---

* This line brings before us the image of the urn into which the ashes were gathered.

The Sire here grant my bones a gentle doom! *
Or, if an Æacus in judgment sit,
Let urn and balls protect me, and acquit.†
Nigh let the brother sit; ‡ and Minos nigh;
And the fell Furies stand as listeners by.
Stop, stone of Sisyphus; Ixion's wheel,
Hush; and let Tantaleus one slow draught steal! §

---

* "The Sire here" is Pluto.

† The "urn and balls," or lot, decided who should sit chief judge in the case. For this judicial custom, see Heyne's Virgil, Æneid, vi. 430, and Excurs. xi. We are not to suppose that the guilt or innocence of the parties arraigned was left to the decision of a lot. And yet Dryden has fallen into this mistake, in his strangely loose version of the Æneid, at the passage referred to: —

> "Round in his urn the blended balls he rolls;
> Absolves the just, and dooms the guilty souls."

‡ "The brother" is Rhadamanthus.

§ Our poet, who rather affects singularities, gives the Greek termination to the name of Tantalus. Ovid has described in the tenth book of the Metamorphoses a similar respite to the sufferings of the tormented ghosts, to Sisyphus, Ixion, and the rest, at the music of Orpheus. The description is familiar to the English reader, through the imitation of it in Pope's "Ode on St. Cecilia's Day." The two Roman poets are at variance, however, in the case of Tantalus. According to Ovid, he ceased to catch at the water, so charmed was he by the sounds of the lyre. Propertius allows him

Let cruel Cerberus scare no ghosts to-day;
And let his unlocked chains their clanking stay!
'T is I my cause that plead; — if aught I feign,
May the poor sisters' vase my shoulders strain! *

If praise in ancient trophies any see,
All Afric speaks Numantine sires for me.†
With this my mother's Albine line may vie,
And lifts my house on twofold titles high.
When soon the maiden robe I ceased to wear,
And bound the bridal ribbon round my hair,
I joined thee, Paulus, — thus to leave thy bed;
Yet write it on my tombstone, But once wed.‡
Witness, O ashes! by thee, Rome, revered,

---

to taste a little, as it flows less rapidly by. The difference seems not wholly unworthy of notice, in an æsthetical point of view.

* Allusion is here made to the punishment of the daughters of Danäus.

† Scipio the younger, surnamed Africanus and Numantinus after he had destroyed Carthage and Numantia, was the ancestor of Cornelia.

‡ Valerius Maximus tells us, that women who took no second husband were held in particular honor. II. 1, 2.

Beneath whose surnames, Afric, thou liest
sheared; —
And he, who laid thy homes, Achilles, bare,
And Perses crushed, Achilles' vaunting heir, —
He, my forefather.* Spotless did I shine,
Nor blushed my hearth for any stain of mine.
Cornelia never shamed such noble birth,
But copied as she could its brightest worth.

Nor did time change me; — pure was all from
blame,
Between the nuptial torch and funeral flame.
Me Nature governed through ingenuous blood,
Lest I should grow, by fear of judgment, good.
Spring from the urn whatever lot austere,†
None sits dishonored by my sitting near.

---

* Æmilius Paulus, surnamed Macedonicus, is meant, who vanquished Perses, the last of the Macedonian kings. These traced their line from Achilles. See the Æneid, vi. 840.

† According to the interpretation given above, this must mean, "Let the most rigorous judge be assigned to me."

Not thou, whose girdle freed the ship aground,
Claudia, chaste priestess of the Turret-crowned;
Nor thou, whose snowy robe relumed the fire,
When Vesta came, her hearth-flame to require.*

Thee I ne'er grieved, dear mother, soon or late.
What wouldst thou wish me changed in, — but
my fate?
Scribonia's tears are praises;† Rome's sad moans,
And Cæsar's sigh, are poured upon my bones.
A sister, worthy his own daughter, dies,‡
And a god's grief flows chiding from his eyes.

But yet I 've worn the matron's prize-array; §

---

* The vestal virgin, Æmilia, whose story is told by Dionysius Hal. and Valerius Max.

† Her mother, Scribonia, became the wife of Augustus Cæsar, and made him the father of the famous Julia.

‡ Cornelia was of course the half-sister of that celebrated beauty whose scandalous life and wretched end appear in singular contrast with the flattering mention of her in this passage, and with the character of her chaste eulogist.

§ There were honorary distinctions for matrons who had borne

Not from a sterile house been snatched away.
Thee, Lepidus! Thee, Paulus! — still my blest!
My dying eyes were closed upon your breast.
My brother twice the curule honors wore; *
I saw him Consul, and then saw no more.
My daughter! image of thy Censor sire, †
Like me, approach but once the marriage fire,
And so sustain thy line. — From the unmoored bark
I shrink not; no more ills my lot shall mark.
O'er the quenched pile when praise is full and free, —
That is the loftiest prize of woman's victory.

---

three children to the state. Frequent mention is made of the "jus trium liberorum" by the Roman writers. What the "vestis honores" here mentioned consisted in, is not, however, very clear.

* P. Cornelius Scipio was ædile and prætor before he arrived at the consulship. These were the required grades of succession.

† Here again is rather an unfortunate instance of praise; for Velleius Paterculus informs us, that the censorship of Plancus and Paulus was spent in quarrels, and was neither honorable to themselves nor useful to the republic; Paulus being wanting in authority, and Plancus in morals. II. 95.

Our sons, love's pledges, now to thee I trust;
This care still breathes, burnt in upon my dust.
Father, fulfil a mother's part; my share
Of the dear burdens now thy neck must bear.
When thou giv'st kisses as they weep, add mine; —
The weight now rests on thee of house and line.
Let them not hear it, when thy sorrows speak;
But kiss them, as they come, with unwet cheek.
Enough the night with thoughts of me to wear,
And dreams, as if my living face was there.
And when thou talk'st, my Paulus, to my shade,
Fancy to each kind word an answer made.
Should e'er an altered bride-bed face the door,*
A step-dame sitting where I sat before,
Your father's choice, my children, bear, — commend;
Subdued by goodness, she will be your friend.

---

* "The nuptial couch was placed in the hall opposite to the door. If it had ever been used for that purpose before, the place of it was changed." — Adam's *Roman Ant.*

Nor praise too much your mother; lest from
thence
A rival feeling kindle to offence.)

Or if content with memories he remain,
My ashes worthy deemed such rank to gain,
Learn how to soothe his age, as on it steals,
And comfort every care the lonely feels.
What fails from mine be in your years enrolled!*
Paulus in you be happy to be old!
All 's well. No mourning weeds the mother
clad,
But every child my funeral farewell bade.

My cause is pleaded. Rise,† ye pitying Powers,
While friendly earth pays back life's honored hours.

---

* This natural and beautiful thought is found also in Martial, at the 37th epigram of the first book: —

"Diceret infernas qui prior îsset ad umbras:
Vive tuo, frater, tempore, — vive meo."

† "Rise," that is, to pronounce your award.

Heaven is unclosed to Worth. Me worthy find,
And bear my bones to rest with their illustrious kind.*

---

* The critical reader will perceive that the conjectural emendation of Heinsius has been adopted in this line. In two other instances, lines 21 and 39, 40, the text of Burmann has been deserted for the more recent one of Kuinoel.

TO-MORROW.

MARTIALIS, V. 58.

To-MORROW, Postumus, you always say, you 'll live;
But when will that to-morrow, Postumus, arrive?
How far off is it? Where? Or how shall it be bid?
Is it somewhere in Parthia or Armenia hid?
To-morrow has already Priam's, Nestor's age.
At what price, say, will it to sell itself engage?
To-morrow, Postumus, you 'll live. — To-day is late.
He who lived yesterday keeps with the wise his state.

MANZONI'S "CINQUE MAGGIO."

THE FIFTH OF MAY.

He was: — and as his latest sigh
 Devoid of motion left
The poor remains, unconscious now,
 Of such a breath bereft, —
So, struck at once aghast and still,
 Stands at the tidings Earth,
Mutely reflecting on that hour,
 The last one of the man of fate;
Nor knows she when another tread
 Of mortal foot, that proud one's mate,
To trample on her bloody dust
 Will spring to birth.

My Genius saw his sparkling throne, —
  Saw, and had naught to say ;
And when in fortune's rapid change
  He fell, — arose, — and lay, —
With thousand voices shouting round,
  It mingled not one cry.
But now, from servile flattery pure,
  From coward insult free,
It rises, — moved that splendor such
  Should fade so suddenly, —
And scatters o'er the urn a chant,
      That may not die.

From the Alps to the Pyramids,
  From the Rhine to the Manzanare,
Of that sure one the thunder-bolt
  Sped with the lightning's glare ; —
He shot from Scylla to the Don,
  From one to the other sea.

Was it true fame ? — For other times
  That high decree. We low
The forehead bend before that Power
  Supreme, which chose to show
What vaster print of its great will
      In him could be.

The stormy and the trembling joy
  Of a grand enterprise, —
The burning care of a tameless heart
  With kingdoms in its eyes, —
Were his ; and then the palm he won
  'T were mad to have hoped from fate.
All he passed through ; — the height of fame
  Heightened by perils o'er, —
The headlong flight, — the victory, —
  The palace, — exile's shore.
Twice was he cast into the dust,
      Twice consecrate.

He named himself; and ages twain,
  Armed with a mutual hate,
Submissively repaired to him,
  As if to know their fate.
He silenced them, and umpire sat,
  Between them, but above.
He vanished; and his vacant months
  Closed on that shore's small bound; —
Object of envy measureless,
  Of pity, too, profound,
Of enmity unquenchable,
      And quenchless love.

As on the head of a wrecked man
  The billow whirls and weighs, —
That billow, o'er whose top the wretch
  Stretches his eager gaze,
Straining his sight, but all in vain,
  To spy the distant land, —

So o'er that mind the foaming weight
Of recollections rolled.
Oft strove he to the times afar
His very self to unfold;
And on the everlasting page
Fell the tired hand.

How often, as the idle day
Was dying into rest,
His flashing looks upon the ground,
His arms across his breast,
He stood; — and of the days that were
Came up the memories thick!
He thought upon the shifting tents,
The rampart's battered force,
The lightning of the infantry,
The surges of the horse,
And of the rapid-spoken order,
Obeyed as quick.

Alas! in such a strife, perhaps,
  The panting spirit fled,
And disappeared; but then a hand
  Strong from the heaven was spread,
And to more respirable air,
  Pitying, that soul conveyed,
And bore it o'er hope's flowery paths
  To everlasting fields,
Where waits that prize whose ready gift
  More than our wishes yields,
And where the fame that passed — is all
    Silence and shade.

Lovely, immortal, bountiful
  Faith, — used to triumph ever!
Write this new victory, and rejoice;
  For haughtier height has never
To the reproach of Golgotha
  Bowed down its humbled crest.

Thou from his weary ashes keep
  Each word that 's harshly spoken!
The God who prostrates and lifts up,
  Who breaks, and heals the broken,
On that lone pillow, at his side
    Vouchsafed to rest.*

---

* Alluding to the crucifix that lay on the death-bed of the Emperor Napoleon.

FROM THE GERMAN.

It may not be improper here to say that the following Translations were made at a time when it was far less common to present the poets of Germany in an English dress than it has since become. There is no one of them in which the writer did not suppose himself to be the first on the field, with the single exception of Von Zedlitz's "Nächtliche Heerschau," of which he had a faint remembrance of a very spirited version read several years before.

GOETHE.

SONG OF THE PARCÆ IN "IPHIGENIA."

IPHIGENIA.

Within my ears resounds that ancient song, —
Forgotten was it, and forgotten gladly, —
Song of the Parcæ, which they shuddering sang,
When Tantalus fell from his golden seat.
They suffered with their noble friend; indignant
Their bosom was, and terrible their song.
To me and to my sisters, in our youth,
The nurse would sing it; and I marked it well.

"The Gods be your terror,
Ye children of men!
They hold the dominion
In hands everlasting,
All free to exert it
As listeth their will.

"Let him fear them doubly
Whome'er they 've exalted!
On crags and on cloud-piles
The couches are planted
Around the gold tables.

"Dissension arises;
Then tumble the feasters,
Reviled and dishonored,
In gulfs of deep midnight;
And look ever vainly
In fetters of darkness
For judgment that 's just.

"But THEY remain seated
At feasts never failing
Around the gold tables.
They stride at a footstep
From mountain to mountain;
Through jaws of abysses
Steams towards them the breathing
Of suffocate Titans,
Like offerings of incense,
A light-rising vapor.

"They turn — the proud masters —
From whole generations
The eye of their blessing;
Nor will in the children,
The once well-beloved,
Still eloquent features
Of ancestor see."

So sang the dark sisters;
The old exile heareth

That terrible music
In caverns of darkness, —
Remembereth his children,
And shaketh his head.

STABILITY IN CHANGE.

Were this early blessing steady,
  Ah, but for a single hour!
But the lukewarm West already
  Shakes abroad a blossom-shower.
Does green Earth my spirit flatter,
  As its first cool shade it throws?
Soon e'en that the storms will shatter,
  Searing it at Autumn's close.

Wouldst thou of the fruits be tasting?
  Haste thy portion soon to get;

Some to their decay are hasting,
  Others in the bud as yet.
All thy pleasant fields are ever
  Changing with each gush of rain;
Ah! and in the selfsame river
  Thou dost never swim again.*

Thou thyself! thou changest, fleest; —
  Rock-firm things that by thee rise,
Walls and palaces, thou seest
  Constantly with different eyes.
Gone from thee the lip that sweetly
  Revelled in the melting kiss,
And the foot that boldly, fleetly
  Scaled, goat-like, the precipice.

Hands that of a frank, kind nature
  Moved but blessings to bestow,

---

* The old Pyrrhonists were fond of this figure.

And the form's symmetric stature, —
  All is turned another now.
And in place of what 's departed,
  That which bears thy name to-day
Hither like a billow darted,
  Then to the Source it speeds away.

Let the end and the beginning
  Draw together into one!
Swifter than what 's round thee spinning,
  Thou thyself be flying on!
Thanks! the Muses' gracious giving
  Makes the Imperishable thine;
In thy breast the Spirit living,
  In thy soul the Form divine.

SCHILLER.

THE OPENING OF THE NEW CENTURY.

1 JANUARY, 1800.

To * * * * *

NOBLE friend! where now for Peace, worn-hearted,
Where for Freedom, is a refuge-place?
For the old century has in storm departed,
And the new with carnage starts its race.

And the bond of nations flies asunder,
And the ancient forms rush to decline;
Not the ocean hems the warring thunder,
Not the Nile-god and the ancient Rhine.

Two imperious nations are contending
  For one empire's universal field;
Liberty from every people rending,
  Thunder-bolt and trident do they wield.

Gold must be weighed them from each country's
      labor;
  And, like Brennus in barbarian days,
See! the daring Frank his iron sabre
  In the balances of Justice lays.

The grasping Briton his trade-fleets, like mighty
  Arms of the sea-polypus, doth spread;
And the realm of unbound Amphitrite
  He would girdle like his own homestead.

To the South-pole's unseen constellations
  Pierce his keels, unhindered, resting not;
All the isles, all coasts of farthest nations,
  Spies he, — all but Eden's sacred spot.

Ah! in vain on charts of all Earth's order
  Mayst thou seek that bright and blessed shore,
Where the green of Freedom's garden border,
  Where man's prime, is fresh for evermore.

Endless lies the world that thine eye traces, —
  Even Commerce scarcely belts it round;
Yet upon its all-unmeasured spaces
  For ten happy ones no room is found.

On the heart's holy and quiet pinion
  Must thou fly from out this rough life's throng;
Freedom lives but within Dream's dominion,
  And the Beautiful blooms but in song.

SIOUX DEATH-SONG.

On the mat he 's sitting there ;
  See ! he sits upright,
With the same look that he ware
  When he saw the light.

Where is now the hands' clenched weight ?
  Where the breath he drew,
That to the Great Spirit late
  Forth the pipe-smoke blew ?

Where the eyes, that, falcon-keen,
  Marked the reindeer pass,
By the dew upon the green,
  By the waving grass ?

These the legs that unconfined
  Bounded through the snow,
Like the stag that 's twenty-tined,
  Like the mountain roe!

These the arms, that stout and tense
  Did the bow-string twang!
See, the life is parted hence!
  See, how loose they hang!

Well for him! he 's gone his ways
  Where are no more snows, —
Where the fields are decked with maize,
  That unplanted grows, —

Where with beasts of chase each wood,
  Where with birds each tree,
Where with fish is every flood
  Stocked full pleasantly.

He above with spirits feeds ; —
  We, alone and dim,
Left to celebrate his deeds,
  And to bury him.

Bring the last sad offerings hither !
  Chant the death-lament !
All inter with him together,
  That can him content.

'Neath his head the hatchet hide,
  That he swung so strong ;
And the bear's ham set beside, —
  For the way is long ; —

Then the knife, — sharp let it be, —
  That from foeman's crown
Quick, with dexterous cuts but three,
  Skin and tuft brought down.

Paints, to smear his frame about,
  Set within his hand,
That he redly may shine out
  In the spirits' land.

CASSANDRA.

Mirth was in old Ilion's halls
  Ere its lofty ramparts fell;
Songs re-echo from the walls,
  With the harp-strings' golden swell.
Warrior hands, the battle done,
  Rest them from the tearful slaughter;
For the royal Peleus' son
  Weds with Priam's beauteous daughter.

To the altar of Apollo,
  'Mid the temple's holiest round,

Crowds on crowds exulting follow,
  Gayly clad and laurel-crowned.
Pouring through the streets of Troy
  Mingling shouts of revel roll;
Severed from the general joy
  Was but one sad, boding soul.

Far from out the revelry
  Did Cassandra joyless rove,
Unattended, silently,
  Through the Thymbrian's laurel grove.
To its farthest, darkest bound
  The prophetic maiden fled,
And cast indignant on the ground
  The fillet from her priestly head.

" All is now on pleasure bent;
  Every heart with rapture fired;
All the elders confident,
  And my sister bride-attired.

None but I must mourn alone,
  For the show deceives not me;
Ruin swift for tower and throne,
  Winged and near, I see, — I see.

"I can see a torch that gleams,
  But not borne by Hymen's hands;
On the clouds a splendor streams,
  Not the light from altar brands.
Feasts I see them gayly spread;
  But my boding spirit hears —
Hears e'en now — a God's stern tread
  Trampling them in blood and tears.

"And they laugh when I complain,
  And they scoff at my distress;
With my bosom's bitter pain
  Must I to the wilderness.
Proud ones shun my solemn mien,
  Light ones mock my prophecy; —

Heavy has thy service been,
  Pythian, thou hard Deity!

"To announce thy fated will,
  Wherefore didst thou cast me here, —
In a city blinded still,
  Slow of heart, and dull of ear?
Wherefore make me prophet-eyed,
  When I cannot change the doom?
What is destined must betide;
  What I shudder at must come.

"Boots it to unveil the terror
  That already threatens nigh?
There is no true life but error;
  To have knowledge is to die.
Shield me from the light I hate;
  Take this bloody show away;
Frightful! thy decree's stern weight
  Pressing on a vase of clay.

"My blest blindness O restore,
  And ignorance, sweet anodyne!
Glad song sung I nevermore
  Since I was a voice of *Thine.*
On my soul the future pours,
  But Thou mak'st the present black;
Spoiled the bliss of passing hours;—
  Take thy faithless present back.

"Never shall the wreath of bride
  Round my fragrant tresses twine,
To thy service sanctified,
  And thy melancholy shrine.
All my youth was but a tear;
  All my knowledge was but smart;
Destinies of kindred dear
  Ever smiting on my heart.

"Merry my companions seem;
  All around me lives and loves,

In the young heart's ardent dream;
  Mine alone but anguish proves.
Vain for me the new-dressed earth,
  Blooming in the Spring's first rays.
Who would prize this life of dearth,
  Could he on its deeps but gaze?

"Ah! Polyxena how blest!
  All her soul a rapture stirs,
Him, of all the Greeks the best,
  Hoping to embrace as hers.
Proud thoughts in her breast arise,
  And their flush she scarce conceals;
She envies not, ye Gods, your skies,
  In the transport that she feels.

"And there 's one, on whom e'en I
  Might my maiden heart bestow;
While his looks plead silently,
  Filled with passion's tenderest glow.

Gladly, as a wife, with him
  Would I seek some home-dear scene ; —
But a Stygian spectre grim
  Nightly starts and stalks between.

" Proserpine from deepest hell
  Sends to me her shades of fright ;
Where I wander, where I dwell,
  Gibbers every ghastly sprite.
O'er the sports of youthful life
  Throw they their infernal stain.
Dreadful, to sustain such strife !
  I shall ne'er have peace again.

" I see gleam the murderous steel ;
  I see burn the murderer's eye ;
Right and left I look, and feel
  From the curse I cannot fly.
Forced to front what I await,
  Knowing, dreading all before,

I must on and end my fate,
  Bleeding on a stranger-shore."

While these words the seer is speaking,
  Hark! from forth the holy fane
Strangely mingled cries are breaking, —
  Thetis' godlike son lies slain.
Eris shakes her snaky brow; —
  All the Gods forsake the place; —
Heavy thunder-clouds hang low
  O'er Trojan towers and Dardan race.

THE FESTIVAL OF ELEUSIS.

Bend to a garland the gold wheat-ear,
  Weave with its kernels its floweret's dye,
Joy from all faces be beaming clear,
  For the Queen herself, the Queen draws nigh;

She, every barbarous passion quelling,
  Making man with his fellow consent,
And into a peaceful, settled dwelling
  Turning his ever-wandering tent.

In the shyest mountain cleft
  Held the Troglodyte abode;
Waste and bare the plains were left,
  Where the roving Nomad trode.
With the arrow, with the bow,
  Ranged the hunter through the land;
Woe betide the stranger, woe!
  Cast upon the luckless strand.

On the search for her lost daughter
  To these coasts, so rude and drear,
Ceres' wandering steps had brought her;
  Ah, no fertile fields appear!
To detain her footsteps there,
  No built roof its welcome rears;

No proud temple's columns fair
  Tell that man the Gods reveres.

No sweet fruits of harvest reach
  For her use their holy food:
Human bones all ghastly bleach
  On the altar's pillar rude.
And where'er her steps she turns,
  Sees she but a fallen fate,
And her generous spirit burns,
  Sorrowing over man's lost state: —

"Is it thus I find his nature,
  Which we cast in our own mould?
Whose divinely modelled stature
  In Olympus we behold?
Gave we not to him the earth
  As a God's grant to possess?
And that realm of regal worth
  Roams he wretched, mansionless?

"Will no God to pity warm?
  None of all the immortal race
Stretch a wonder-working arm,—
  Lift him from his deep disgrace?
In their heavenly, blest domain
  They are dull to others' smart;
Yet does human dearth and pain
  Reach and wring my troubled heart.

"If man would become man's brother,
  Let him be in compact bound
Cordial with his pious Mother,
  With the all-sustaining Ground.
Let him honor Seasons, Times,
  Trace the Moon's pure course along;
Their calm movement ever chimes
  One melodious, endless song."

Then she softly bursts the cloud
  That detained her from their sight,

And at once, 'mid that wild crowd,
  Stands revealed, — a form of light!
Hot were they with feast and slaughter,
  When among their horde she stood,
And their savage shell they brought her
  Frothing with their foemen's blood.

Horror thrilled her frame the while,
  And she turned away her head.
" Bloody tiger-meals defile
  Ne'er a God's pure lips," she said;
" Stainless offerings are our pleasure,
  Fruitage which the fields afford;
With the Autumn's harvest treasure
  Will the Holy be adored."

And she takes the spear-staff's weight
  From the hunter's rugged hand;
With its point of deadly fate
  Furrows she the yielding sand;

Plucks from out her bearded crown
  One small grain of hidden might;
Sinks it in its small trench down,
  And it swells and shoots to light.

And with green blade instantly
  Does the ground its breadth adorn,
And as far as eye can see
  Waves like golden boughs the corn.
Smiling blesses she the Earth,
  The first gathered sheaf she binds,
Plants the field-stone for a hearth;
  Utterance then the Goddess finds:—

"Father Jupiter, who reignest
  O'er all Gods in upper air!
That to accept our gift thou deignest,
  Let some omen now declare.
And from this ill-fated race,
  Who thy name have never known,

Loftiest! every dark cloud chase,
  That they may the Godhead own."

And his sister's earnest cry
  Comes before the high-throned Sire;
Thundering from the clear blue sky
  Flies his bolt of jagged fire.
Now the altar, crackling bright,
  Forth its whirling columns pours;
With them, wheeled in circling light,
  Up his swift-winged eagle soars.

To the feet of the Goddess with raptured devotion
  The multitude press and bend the knee,
And their rough souls melt with glad emotion
  In the first warm gush of humanity.
And away they throw the murderous steel,
  And open their darkly-fastened mind,
And the heavenly teaching receive and feel
  From the queenly Friend of human kind.

From the throne of his domain
  Straight descends each helpful God;
Themis leads the immortal train,
  In her hand the righteous rod;
And she metes to each his right;
  Plants herself the boundary stone;
And the Styx's mystic might
  Calls to witness what is done.

From amidst the forge's blaze
  Comes the inventive son of Jove;
Founder he of figured vase,
  Brass and clay his skill approve.
And how to clinch the tongs he shows,
  To blow the breathing bellows, how;
Beneath his hammer's clanging blows
  First of all comes forth the plough.

And Minerva, high o'er all,
  Wields her spear of ponderous might,

And with her majestic call
  Guides the heavenly throng aright.
Walls she rears with deep foundations,
  For a refuge and defence,
To enclose the scattered nations,
  Bound in mutual confidence.

As her regal steps she bends
  O'er the landscape's ample rounds,
Closely at her side attends
  Terminus, the God of Bounds.
And the chain's dividing thread
  Round the hills' green skirts she throws,
And the torrent's wildest bed
  Girds within the sacred close.

All the nymphs of cliff and fountain,
  Who Diana's bidding hear,
Following her through grove and mountain,
  Brandishing their hunting-spear, —

All are coming, all uniting
  In the work ; their shouts resound,
And before their axes' smiting
  Crash the pine woods to the ground.

From his mossy source remote
  Rousing him, the sedge-crowned God
Rolls the heavy raft afloat
  At the Goddess' potent nod.
Kirtled high, and light for duty,
  Fly the Hours, an eager band,
And the rough trunks grow to beauty,
  Rounded by their busy hand.

And the Sea-God hastens on ;
  With his trident's rapid shock,
From the ribbed earth's skeleton
  Breaks he loose the granite block.
And his giant arms in air
  Toss it lightly as a ball ;

Then, with Hermes' skilful care,
  Ramparts he the well-fenced wall.

And from out his golden strings
  Phœbus draws sweet harmony,
Time's delightful measurings,
  And the might of melody;
While the Muses' nine-tongued choir
  Blend their voices' magic tone,
Till at sound of voice and lyre
  Stone in concert moves to stone.

Folding gates with leaves so vast
  Hangs the experienced Cybele;
And she fits them iron-fast
  With the lock's strong ministry.
Quick the wonder-pile 's complete,
  Built by nimble hands divine;
And, for pomp of worship meet,
  Bright the Temple's glories shine.

With a myrtle crown again
  Comes the Queen of Gods to bless;
And she leads the comeliest swain
  To the loveliest shepherdess.
Venus with her beauteous boy
  Decks, herself, the youthful pair;
All the Gods bring gifts of joy,
  Blessing the first-wedded there.

Ushered by that troop immortal,
  Now the new-made People throng
Guest-like through the open portal,
  Music charming them along.
Ceres at the altar stands,
  And the priestly offering pays,
Blessing with her folded hands;
  Then to all aloud she says: —

" Freedom is the beasts' wild pleasure;
  Free the God in ether reigns;

Their fixed nature is the measure
  That their fiery wills restrains.
Less than Gods, — of brutes the betters, —
  Men with men close-bound should be;
Only as their Duty's debtors
  Are they strong, or are they free."

Bend to a garland the gold wheat-ear,
  Weave with its kernels its flower's * blue dye;
Joy from all faces be beaming clear,
  For the Queen herself, the Queen draws nigh.
She who has given us home and brother,
  Making man with his fellow consent!
To her, the all-propitious Mother,
  The song of our ceaseless praise be sent!

---

* The Cyané.

THE FLOWERS.

Children of the Sun's new splendor,
  Flowers of the enamelled Earth,
Born fresh gifts and joys to render,
  Nature loved you at your birth!
Broidered rays, a robe, surround you,
Flora has with beauty crowned you,
  Heavenly pomp of colors bright.
Spring-born! weep for one thing wanted;
Soul the Goddess has not granted;
  For yourselves you dwell in night.

Nightingale and lark are singing
  To you love's delicious haps;
Tricksy Sylphids, too, are flinging
  Rival forms into your laps.

When Dione's daughter moulded
Your arched cups, she surely folded
 Love's own swelling pillow there.
Mourn, ye Spring-born, that for ever
Love and you are doomed to sever,
 And its bliss you cannot share!

But when mother-words, stern spoken,
 Banish me from Nannie's view,
And as tender pledge and token
 I am seeking, gathering you, —
Then life, speech, heart, soul-expression,
Heralds dumb of sour-sweet passion,
 Through you pours this touch of mine;
And the Chief of heavenly powers
In your silent leaves, ye flowers,
 Wraps his energy divine.

A DITHYRAMB.

NEVER, believe me,
Appear the Divine Ones,
Never alone.
Scarce have I Bacchus, the wakener of joy,
But Love is there also, the laughing young boy;
Phœbus the Lordly consents to make one.
They 're coming, they 're near us,
The Deities all,
With Gods is now filling
The poor, earthly hall.

Say, how can I take,
Child of the earth here,
Guests from on high?
Grant me, like you, ye Gods, deathless to live!

What offering for you hath a mortal to give?
Up to Olympus O help me to fly!
Joy dwells only
Where Deities sup.
O fill me the nectar!
O reach me the cup!

Reach him the cup!
Pour for the bard,
Hebe, pour free!
Sprinkle his eyesight with heaven's bedewing,
That the Styx, the detested, he may not be viewing,
But one of ourselves may suppose him to be!
It gushes, it sparkles,
The fount of the skies!
How peaceful the bosom!
How radiant the eyes!

SAYINGS OF CONFUCIUS.

I.

The steps of Time have a threefold gait:—
Loitering slow, the Future advances;
Arrow-swift by, the Present glances;
Ever the Past holds its fixed estate.
No impatient thought can wing it,
When its lingering feet delay;
Fear nor doubt to pause can bring it,
As it speeds away,—away;
Nor magic charm, nor guilt's distress,
Avails to move the Motionless.

Wouldst thou with the blest and wise
End the course that before thee lies?
Let the Loiterer counsel read,
But ne'er be partner to thy deed;
Do not a friend with the Flying one go,
Nor make the Unchangeable one thy foe.

II.

Threefold is the form of SPACE.
Length sets on with steady race,
Restless far and forward leading;
Boundless, *Breadth* is each side spreading;
Fathomless does *Depth* descend.

These are emblems to thee granted.
Forward still must thou undaunted,
Never tired or standing still,
Wouldst thou thy true end fulfil;
Must thyself in Breadth unfold,
Wouldst thou the world's image hold;
Into Depth must see to go,
If Existence thou wouldst know.
Wouldst reach the goal, then persevere;
Only in Fulness art thou clear;
Only low down will Truth appear.

HERDER.

ODE TO THE HEBREW PROPHETS.

PREFIXED TO THE THIRD VOLUME OF EICHHORN'S INTRODUCTION TO THE OLD TESTAMENT.

O TRUSTY ones of God! I bend and greet you.
Rest ye at last within your grove of palms,
A rest which Horeb, Zion, Carmel, gave not?
How do your early times stand debtors to you!
For laws, religion, morals, sacred hopes,
The weal of states, the precepts of the wise,
All flowed like blessed fountains from your lips.
For yours were noble spirits, that soared up
Beyond the sluggish present, and the dreams

Of a subjected and a doting people,
Above each common joy, each fond illusion,
And back and forward saw the light of ages.
Far onward, far behind, that light was beaming,
And your souls felt it like the fire of heaven.
Long burned the flame in still obscurity,
Then shone to illume the course of days yet distant.

In holy shades of solitude ye listened
In rapt obedience to the unearthly voice,
Which at the midnight or the dawning hour
Stole o'er the heart and waked its finest chords.
Now softly fell the tones like showers in Spring;
Now swept like tempests o'er a slumbering world,
As if the thousand voices of the past
And of all coming times were mingling there.

Ye true and pure of soul! again I greet you;
Ye harp-strings in the hands of Deity;

Interpreters of Heaven; life of the laws;
And heralds of events that yet appeared not!
O thou of Sinai, who midst cloud and storm,
Leaving the world and thy dark age beneath
thee,
Didst look upon that splendor which now spreads
Its glories round the earth, and on the form
Of wisdom decked with pomp and bright with
wonders!
Thou soul of flame which snatched from heaven
its fires,
And from the realm of shades the widow's son!
Thou who didst see Jehovah on his throne,
With all the glittering train that filled his temple!
Ye mournful ones, who sang but to lament,
And poured in tears your gentle hearts away!
And ye, who in the evening of the prophets
Saw through the twilight dusky forms advance!
Ye all, who, now to happier regions risen,
Your labors ceased and every conflict ended,

Roam through your grove of palms, and taste of
    rest, —
A rest which Horeb, Zion, Carmel, gave not!

What do I see? Who join themselves to these
So brotherly? The wise of other nations?
Yes, the select of God through all the world;
The noble company of Druid sages;
Plato and Orpheus and Pythagoras;
All who were e'er the fathers of the people
And guardians of the laws; who faithfully
Bowed a pure ear to catch the voice of Heaven,
Gave a pure heart to feel its inspiration.

RÜCKERT.

THE DYING FLOWER.

Hope! Thou yet shalt live to see
Vernal sun and vernal air;
Such the hope of every tree
Stript by Autumn's tempests bare.
Hidden in their quiet strength,
Winter-long their germs repose,
Till the sap starts fresh at length,
And the new-born verdure grows.

"Ah! no mighty tree am I,
That a thousand summers lives,

And, its winter dream gone by,
Spring-like green and gladness gives.
I am but an humble flower
Wakened by the kiss of May;
There is left no trace of power,
As shrouded white I drop away."

Since thou then a floweret art,
Modest child of gentle kin,
Hear thou this, and so take heart: —
Every plant has seed within.
Be it that the wind of death
Scatters thee with blast and cold;
Still thou 'lt breathe in other's breath,
Thus renewed a hundredfold.

"Yes, as I shall but have been,
Others like me soon shall be;
Endless is the general green, —
Single leaves die presently.

Be they all I used to show; —
I can be myself no more;
All my being lives in *now*,
Naught behind and naught before.

" Though the sun, that warms me yet,
Dart through *them* his glances bright;
That soothes not the fate that 's set,
Dooming me to endless night.
Sun! already them that follow
Followest thou with glowing eye;
Mock me not with that dim, hollow,
Frosty glance from clouded sky!

" Woe 's me, that I felt thy blaze
Kindling me to my short day!
That I met thy ardent gaze
Till it stole my life away!
What of that poor life remains
From thy pity I 'll withhold;

I 'll avoid thee, — and my pains
Close in my closed self upfold.

"Yet these icy thoughts relent,
Melted by thee to a tear; —
Take, O take my breath that 's spent,
Everlasting, to thy sphere!
Yes; thou sunnest all the sorrow
Out from my dark heart at last;
Dying, all I had to borrow
I thank thee for, — now all is past.

"For every gentle note of Spring;
Each Summer's gale I trembled to;
Each golden insect's dancing wing,
That gayly round my leaflets flew;
For eyes that sparkled at my hues;
For hearts that blest my fragrancy; —
Made but of tints and odorous dews,
Maker, I still give thanks to thee.

"Of thy world an ornament,
Though a trifling and a poor,
I to grace the fields was sent,
As stars bedeck their higher floor.
One gasp have I left me still,
And no sigh shall that be found;
One look yet to heaven's high hill
And the beauteous world around.

"Let me towards thee pour my soul,
Fire-heart of this lower sphere!
Heaven! thine azure tent unroll; —
Mine, once green, hangs wrinkled here.
Hail, O Spring, thy beaming eye!
Hail, O Morn, thy wooing breath!
Without complaint in death I lie,
If without hope to rise from death."

STRUNG PEARLS.

'T is true, the breath of sighs throws mist upon a
mirror;
But yet, through breath of sighs the soul's clear
glass grows clearer.
From God there is no flight, but only *to* Him.
Daring
Protects not when He frowns, but the child's filial
bearing.
The father feels the blow when he corrects his son;
But when thy heart is loose, rigor 's a kindness
done.
A father should to God pray, each new day at
latest,
"Lord, teach me how to use the power thou dele-
gatest!"
O look, whene'er the world thy senses would be-
tray,

Up to the steady heavens, where the stars never
stray.
The sun and moon take turns, and each to each
gives place;
Else were e'en their wide house but a too narrow
space.
When thy weak heart is tossed with passion's fiery
gust,
Say to it, " Knowest thou how soon thou shalt be
dust?"
Say to thy foe, " Is death not common to us
twain?
Come then, death-kinsman mine, and we'll be
friends again."
Much rather than the spots upon the Sun's broad
light,
Would Love spy out the Stars scarce twinkling
through the night.
Thou none the better art for seeking what to
blame,

And ne'er wilt famous be by blasting others' fame.
The name alone remains when all beside is reft ;
O leave, then, to the dead that little which is left !
Repentance can avail from God's rebuke to save ;
But men will ne'er forget thine errors in thy grave.
Be good, and fear for naught that slanderous speech endangers ;
Who bears no sin himself affords to bear a stranger's.
Say to thy pride, " 'T is all but ashes for the urn ;
Come, let us own our dust, before to dust we turn."
Be yielding to thy foe, and peace shall he yield back ;
But yield not to thyself, and thou 'rt on victory's track.
Who is thy deadliest foe ? — An evil heart's desire,
Which hates thee still the worse, as thy weak love mounts higher.
Know'st thou where neither lords nor wretched serfs appear ?

Where one the other serves, for each to each is
dear.
Thou 'lt ne'er arrive at love, while still to life
thou 'lt cling;
I 'm found but at the cost of thy self-offering.
According as thou wouldst receive, thou must
impart;
Must wholly give a life, to wholly have a heart.

Till thought of thine own worth far buried from
thee lies,
How know I that indeed *my* worth 's before thine
eyes?
What more says he that speaks, than he who
holds his peace?
Yet woe betide the heart that from thy praise can
cease!
Say I, "In thee I am"? — Say I, "Thou art in
me"? —
Thou art what in me is; — what I am is through
thee.

O sun, I am thy beam; O rose, I am thy scent;
I am thy drop, O sea; thy breath, O firmament!
Unmeasured mystery! what not the heavens contain
Will here be held in this small heart and narrow brain.
Of that tree I'm a leaf, which ever new doth sprout;
Hail me! my stock remains though winds toss me about.
Destruction blows on thee, while thou alone dost stay;
O feel thee in that whole which ne'er shall pass away!
How great soe'er thyself, thou 'rt naught before the All;
But, as a member there, important though most small.
The little bee to fight doth like a champion spur,
Because, not for herself, she feels her tribe in her;

Because so sweet her work, so sharp must be her
sting;
The earth hath no delight unscourged of suffering.
From the same flower she sucks both food and
poison up;
For death doth lurk alway in life's delicious cup.
The mulberry-leaf must bear the biting of a worm,
That so it may be raised to wear its silken form.
See, how along the ground the ant-hosts blindly
throng!
Yet no more than the choirs of stars can these go
wrong.
Toward setting sun the lark floats on in jubilee;
Frisking in light, the gnat to himself makes
melody.
Sundown;—the lark's note melts into the air of
even;
To earth she falls not back; her grave is in the
heaven.
When twilight fades, steal forth the constellations
bright;

Below, 't is Day that lives, — in upper air, the
Night.
The powerful sun to earth the fainting spirit beats,
Which mounts again on night's sweet breath of
violets.
Through heaven, the livelong night, I'm floating
in my dreams,
And when I rouse, my room a scanty limit seems.
Wake up! The sun presents an image in his
rays,
How man can shine at morn to his Creator's
praise.
Cups of all various hues do the new wine contain,
With which King Spring comes forth to feast his
courtier train.
The Lily with seven tongues her conscious bravery
shows;
With bud-lips half-way open, silent stands the
Rose.
The Tulip-bed doth reel, drunk with its beauty's
fame;

Who cares to count each spark, when Love is all in flame? —
Narcissus, turning to thee the star of her golden eye,
Says: "As I towards the light, look thou towards God on high."
The flowers all tell to thee a sacred, mystic story,
How moistened earthy dust can wear celestial glory.
On thousand stems is found the love-inscription graven:
"How beautiful is earth, when it can image heaven!"
Wouldst thou first pause to thank thy God for every pleasure,
For mourning over griefs thou wouldst not find the leisure.
O heart! but try it once; — 't is easy good to be,
But to appear so, such a strain and misery.
Who hath his day's work done, may rest him as he will;

O, quick, then, urge thyself thy day's work to
fulfil!
Of what each one should be, before him lies the
rule;
Till he comes up with that, his joy can ne'er be
full.
O, pray for life! thou feel'st that, with these faults
of thine,
Thou art not ready yet with sons of God to shine.
From the sun's searching power can vagrant plan-
ets rove?
How then can wandering man fall wholly from
God's love?
Still from each circle's point to the centre lies a
track;
And there's a way to God from furthest error back.
Whoso mistakes me now, but spurs me on to
make
My life so speak henceforth that no one can mis-
take.

And though throughout the world the good I nowhere find,
I still have faith in it, for its image in my mind.
The heart that holds to love is not abandoned yet;
The smallest fibre serves some root in God to set.
So strong is Love's dear might, God will himself submit,
And where He is beloved, bows His own might to it;
Yea, fears not lest through Love Himself should stoop too low; —
How should not I the love I find, in turn bestow?
From the worse smart of guilt correction sets thee free;
Thou art not chastened, child, through wrath, but clemency.
Since Love would quicken thee to life, be like the ground!
Not out of stubborn flint will Spring's soft growths be found.

Because she bears the pearl, — that makes the
oyster sore; —
Be thankful for the pain that but exalts thee more.
The sweetest fruit grows not when the tree's sap
is full;
The Spirit is not ripe till meaner powers grow
dull.
The air consumes itself in the last love-sigh it
gave;
To God's breath then transformed, it wakes life
from the grave.
Spring weaves a magic net of odors, colors, sounds;
Come, Autumn! free the soul from these enchanted
bounds.
My tree was thick with shade: O Blast! thine
office do,
And strip the foliage off, to let the heavens shine
through.
They 're wholly blown away, bright blossoms and
green leaves; —

They 're brought home to the barn, all colorless,
the sheaves.
O Tree of Life! behold, the Fall-gale shakes thee
now,
To search if fruit is hid beneath thy well-clothed
bough.
Rejoice thou at the proof, who art not barren seen;
And shudder thou, with naught but that proud
leafy screen.
The swallow leaves her nest, and seeks a warmer
clime;
O Soul, soar thou up too! 'T is the Earth's
Winter-time.
My heart pines for that Spring, which dreads no
icy storm;
For the Rose, whose breast is stung by neither
thorn nor worm.
I know the Garden well, where all those Summers
stay
Which through these rolling zones such flying
visits pay.

I know the Garden well, that ne'er its growths denied;
Where all is borne as fruit, that here as blossom died.
A fragment is my song, and so is that of the earth,
Which hopes in a farther land to find its finished worth.
The Love, that high in heaven clusters the Pleiades,
Holds on invisible threads even such Pearls as these.

A GAZELLE.*

Nightingales of Spring were singing, how long
ago!
And roses in the fields were springing, how long
ago!
The ruddy Morn her bloody banners, every new
day,
Anew across the Earth was flinging, how long ago!
Stars within the concave heaven, and sun and
moon,
Before men's eyes their course were winging, how
long ago!
And to men's eyes, as to the flowers, has passing
time
Their opening and their close been bringing, how
long ago!

---

* This name denotes merely a peculiar measure of verse.

And to the hearts of men, as life swelled them with breath,
Came hope's delight and sorrow's stinging, how long ago!
And fame and lordship — soapy bubbles in the sun's blaze —
Were rounding bright, asunder springing, how long ago!
And over earth's and heaven's limits, nobly aloft,
The Spirit's boundless wish was swinging, how long ago!
The Soul, that through the soul of beauty hopes to be free,
Feels low joys lording it and kinging, how long ago!
A beam from heaven has smitten me, dimming the shine
Of all the world's poor spangle-stringing, how long ago!
Lost to the echo is the forum's noise in this breast,

Where thine all-silent words were ringing, how long ago!
No lure for me have Fortune's nets upon life's road;
I rest among thine elf-locks clinging, how long ago!

QUATRAINS,

IN THE PERSIAN MANNER.

I.

O, BE in God's clear world no dark and troubled sprite!
To Christ, thy master mild, do no such foul despite;
But show in look, word, mien, that thou belong'st to him,
Who says, "My yoke is easy, and my burden light."

II.

So long as life's hope-sparkle glows, 't is good;
When death delivers from life's woes, 't is good.
O praise the Lord, who makes all good and well!
Whether He life or death bestows, 't is good.

III.

The stars above me mount the heavens with tranquil beam;
So round my couch, O Lord, may heavenly warders gleam!
And if my bolster be, like Jacob's, a hard stone,
Let Jacob's ladder, too, be lifted in my dream!

IV.

There came from heaven a flying turtle-dove,
And brought a leaf of clover from above;
He dropped it, — and O happy they that find!
The triple flower is Faith and Hope and Love.

AL-SIRAT.

'Twixt Time and Eternity
  Stands the Bridge of Doom;
Filling with fierce radiancy
  The dread chasm's gloom.

Know'st thou well, how sharp and fine
  That bridge arches there?
Sharp as any sword its line,
  Fine as any hair.

Shall the foot of man be set
  On a bridge so thin,
Where no room a fly could get
  To find footing in?

He that does not firmly dare
  Trust himself on this,
Must not hope beyond to share
  Eden's dewy bliss.

When the wicked o'er it goes,
  Stands the bridge all sparkling;
And his mind bewildered grows,
  And his eye swims darkling.

Wakening, giddying, then comes in,
  With a deadly fright,
Memory of all his sin
  Rushing on his sight.

Underneath him gapes the chasm;—
  Conscience, desperate grown,
Drives him with its maddening spasm
  To plunge headlong down.

But when forward steps the just,
He is safe e'en here ; —
Round him gathers holy trust,
And drives back his fear.

Hope is lifting up his brow,
Love is giving wings ;
Faith is smiling, as he now
On so happy springs.

Each good deed 's a mist, that wide,
Golden borders gets ;
And for him the bridge, each side,
Shines with parapets.

Onward still his footsteps fare,
And the bridge is passed,
As 't were built of stones hewn square,
Or of iron cast.

Freimund![*] at that pass, thy lays
Thus around thee sweep
Mistful! — that thou mayst not gaze
Down the dizzy deep.

Floating like the morning wind
O'er the lilies' bed
Move, and ever lightly mind
On the bridge to tread.

THE VALUE OF YEARS.

Adam sat in Paradise circled by many a spirit, —
All souls of those, that, as time flows, should come
this life to inherit.

[*] The name which Rückert adopted as his *nom de plume* in his earlier writings.

God the Lord brought each before the great forefather's face,
That what was written on their fronts his prophet
eye might trace.
Letters bright on every brow, drawn by the heavenly finger,
Showed the number of the years that each in life
should linger.

Adam said: "Who is the man that nobly now
advances?
A minstrel's fire is on his lips, a seer's in his
glances."
"That is David," said the Lord, "thy son, the
pious king;
Wondrous gifts his heart inspire, that he my
praise should sing."
"And but sixty years," said Adam, "are to him
appointed?
Give twice twenty of my thousand to thine own
anointed!"

The wish of our first parent was answered: "Be it done;
And give the years twice twenty to Jesse's youngest son."

Adam far from Paradise his fallen years had passed,
And the dread death-angel came to bury him at last.
"What wilt thou here?" cried Adam, and with angry eye;
"Forty of my thousand years are due before I die."
But the angel said: "Not so; I come not a day too soon;
Forgettest thou that forty become King David's boon?"
"Alas!" sighed Adam; "then I sat within my Eden-bowers;—
The boon should not be valid on the earth that now is ours."

Freimund, Adam's son! reflect, that none in Eden's bliss
Know how much a year is worth in an earth-lot like this.

SOLOMON AND THE SOWER.

In open field King Solomon
Beneath the sky sets up his throne;
He sees a sower walking, sowing,
On every side the seed-corn throwing.

"What dost thou there?" exclaimed the king;
"The ground here can no harvest bring.
Break off from such unwise beginning;
Thou 'lt get no crop that 's worth the winning."

The sower hears ; his arm he sinks,
And doubtful he stands still, and thinks ;
Then goes he forward, strong and steady,
For the wise king this answer ready : —

" I've nothing else but this one field ;
I've watched it, labored it, and tilled.
What further use of pausing, guessing ?
The corn from me, — from God the blessing."

—◆—

FROM THE YOUTH-TIME.

From my youthful day, from my youthful day,
Comes a song with ceaseless tone ;
O how far away, O how far away,
What *was* my own !

What the swallow sung, what the swallow sung,
Bringing the harvests and the spring,
Village fields among, village fields among,
Does she still sing ? —

" When I left the plain, when I left the plain,
Heavy the bin and full the stall ;
When I came again, when I came again,
'T was empty all."

O mouth of childhood gay ! mouth of childhood gay !
All unconsciously wise one !
You know what the birds say, know what the birds say,
Like Solomon.

O thou dear home-floor ! O thou dear home-floor !
Again within thy sacred bound
Let me yet once more, let me yet once more
In dreams be found !

When I left the plain, when I left the plain,
The Earth to me was Plenty's hall; —
When I came again, when I came again,
'T was empty all.

The swallow will come back; the swallow will come back;
The empty crib its store regains; —
When the heart comes to lack, when the heart comes to lack,
Void it remains.

Back no swallow brings, back no swallow brings,
What thou sighest for so sore;
Yet the swallow sings, yet the swallow sings,
Just as before: —

"When I left the plain, when I left the plain,
Heavy the bin and full the stall;
When I came again, when I came again,
'T was empty all."

THE OLD MAN'S SONG.

FROM THE "ÖSTLICHEN ROSEN."

[The Song may be sung to the original music by SCHUBERT.]

MY dwelling's roof with service is frosted o'er,
Yet warm are all the chambers, e'en as of yore.
My head the Winter covers, all white and hoar;
Yet through the heart's free portals life's red tides
 pour.
 The blooms of youth are vanished;
 The cheeks' bright roses banished;
 One by one they were seen no more.
 Where have they thus been going? —
 To my heart's core.
 There to my wish they 're blowing
 Just as before.

The streams of worldly pleasure, are they all dry?
Still one calm stream is laving that inner shore.

The nightingales of Summer, did they all die?
Still one, amid the silence, my thoughts restore.
She sings: "Lord, close the mansion, I now implore,
That the old world intrude not within the door!
Shut out the reeky breathing of things called real
But give to dreams ideal
Both roof and floor."

THE NOURISHER.

I AM the Spirit, that all life do feed;
Through all creation's realms I breathe and flow
With nurture manifold; — take what you need!
A poisonous stream, I penetrate below
Earth's rifts and chasms; thou stiff and shapeless ore,

Suck up the damp, that thou to form mayst
grow!
A rushing spring, my stream I upwards pour;
O plant, that forth thy silent life dost shoot,
Nor pained, nor glad, imbibe thy vital store!
O beast, afoam with greed and passions brute,
Devour the spoil of the earth's stupid crust,
Till thou thyself art stupid as thy fruit!
Now quit thy well-gnawed leaf, dull worm, thou
must,
Then wing thyself into a butterfly,
And drink in, dying, the pure blossom-dust!

But Thou, not doomed within earth's rounds to lie,
Lift up thyself, O Human Countenance,
And take the spirit-food that I supply!
Receive the Night's deep tone, the day's bright
glance,
And shape them in thyself to light and song;
Through eye and tongue then give them utterance.

Let my air's breath within thee flow along!
Thou dost inhale the heaven in breathing this,
And breathest back to heaven its current strong.
Thou sipp'st my wine in love's enamored kiss;
And when the exchanging transport mingles souls,
Each must to each become a food of bliss.
From earthly pits the tide of pleasure rolls;
The grape's juice for the noble banquet streams,
And Inspiration dipp'st thou up in bowls.
More! From on high come trembling down my
beams,
And kindle in thy thought its nourishment,
With that sweet parch of thirst which souls be-
seems.
Much as thou drinkest, more will less content,
Till satisfied is all thy longing fire,
By blending with the Source from which 't was
sent; —
For death alone can feed thy full desire.

A GAZELLE.

LIFE's ills end well upon Death's bed;
Yet Life shrinks back from Death with dread.
Life sees but the dark hand, and not
The clear cup that it holds, instead.
So shrinks the heart from Love away,
As if 't were thus to ruin led.
And truly when Love fully wakes,
The gloomy despot Self lies dead.
So let it perish in the night,
And breathe thou free the morning's red.

MOTHER SUN.

BY a singular anomaly, the Sun is feminine, and the Moon masculine, in German. "Mundilfori had two children; a son Mani (Moon) and a daughter Sôl (Sun)," says the Prose Edda.

THE Mother Sun is heard, —
A sunbeam every word, —

To her little children speaking:
"What would ye now be seeking?

"Why in such haste away
From my warm breast to stray?
For scarcely can my glances
Reach you in your wide dances.

"My youngster, Mercury, fleet
With wings upon thy feet!
Of all my seven thou fliest
Still to thy mother nighest.

"Thy form thou dippest quite
Beneath my flood of light;
And they who move remotest
Scarce spy thee where thou floatest.

"My Venus, maiden fair!
Of curly gold thy hair;

With rays the world adorning,
At even and at morning.

"O Jupiter and Mars,
Kingly and warrior stars!
What pomp ye bear before ye,
Equipped in burning glory!

"Saturn and Uranus!
Ye cause a pain to us,
That, last in our bright order,
Ye choose the outmost border.

"O Earth, my darling child!
From out thy bosom mild
Thou bringest the subjection
That best meets my affection

"Not too far, — not too nigh, —
The apple of my eye!

Of all my looks, the clearest
Rest on thy face, my dearest!

" Forth from the beams I spread
Thou weav'st the morning's red;
How rich the purple binding
Around thy tresses winding!

" Then from the cloud's thin lawn
Thy silver veil is drawn;
The rainbow, sevenfold splendid,
For thy robe's hem is bended.

" Thy diligence I see;
How, as a gift for me,
Thou broiderest and paintest,
Cheering my eye when faintest.

" My single golden ray
How hast thou found the way

So many hues to furnish,
Thy tapestries to burnish?

" And all thy flowers, in pride,
Ruby and sapphire dyed,
Soon as my warmth I proffer,
Their kindled incense offer.

" Thou mak'st the drops of dew
A rustic mirror true ;
My image there appearing,
In tints of richest wearing.

" With thousand eyes new-born
Thou art awake at morn,
And from mine eyes derivest
The light by which thou livest.

" Then postest thou at night
The moon upon his height ;

He is thine own creation,
Thy choice his warder-station.

" He watches in his place,
Still fixed on mine his face;
His flag for thee erected,
His beams from me reflected.

" ANOTHER child is brought
Forth from thine earnest thought,
Which in thy bosom ponders,
And looks at me, and wonders.

" When he has sought thee out,
With spirit keen and stout,
And me, too, studied throughly, —
Then all will finish duly.

" Then wilt thou flash out free
Thine inward radiancy, —

The lightning-thought all burning,
Each gloomy barrier spurning.

" So onward think and fare: —
And all you others there,
Swing round me in glad measures,
And please me with your pleasures.

"You cannot from me part,
Whatever way you start;
My gold cord holds you, rangers,
And keeps you from all dangers.

" And when ye have attained
Whereto ye were ordained,
Come to this breast of fire,
And buried there expire."

BETHLEHEM AND GOLGOTHA.

In Bethlehem He first arose,
From whom we draw our true life's breath;
And Golgotha at last He chose,
Where his cross broke the power of death.
I wandered from the Western strand,
Through strange scenes of the Morning Land;
But naught so great did I survey
As Bethlehem and Golgotha.

The ancient wonders of the world
Here rose aloft, — the mighty Seven; —
How was their transient glory hurled
To earth before the might of Heaven!
In passing, I could see and tell
How all their pride to ruin fell;
There stood in quiet Gloria
But Bethlehem and Golgotha.

Cease, Pyramids of Egypt, cease!
The toil that built you never gave
The faintest thought of Death's great peace, —
'T was but the darkness of a grave.
Ye Sphinxes, in colossal stone!
The riddle Life an unread one
Ye left; — the answer found its way
Through Bethlehem and Golgotha.

O Rocknabad, earth's Paradise,
Of all Shiraz the sweetest flower!
Ye Indian sea-coasts, breathing spice,
Where groves of palms in beauty tower; —
I see o'er all your sunny plains
The step of Death leave sable stains.
Look up! There comes a deathless ray
From Bethlehem and Golgotha.

Thou Cāāba! black stone of the waste,
At which the feet of half our line

Yet stumble. Stand, now, proudly braced
Beneath thy crescent's waning shine!
The moon before the sun grows dim;—
Thou art shattered by the sign of Him,
The conquering Prince. "Victoria!"
Shout Bethlehem and Golgotha.

O Thou, who in a shepherd-stable
An infant willingly hast lain,
And through the cross's pain wert able
To give the victory over pain!
To pride the manger seems disgrace;
The cross a vile, unworthy place;—
But what shall bring this pride down? Say!
'T is Bethlehem and Golgotha.

The Magi kings went forth to see
The Shepherd Stock, the Paschal Lamb;
And to the cross on Calvary
The pilgrimage of nations came.

Amidst the battle's stormy toss,
All flew to splinters — but the Cross ;
As East and West encamping lay
Round Bethlehem and Golgotha.

O, march we not in martial band,
But with the Spirit's flag unfurled!
Let us subdue the Holy Land
As Christ himself subdued the world.
Let beams of light on every side
Fly, like Apostles, far and wide,
Till all men catch the beams that play
O'er Bethlehem and Golgotha.

With pilgrim staff and scallop-shell
Through Eastern climes I sought to roam;
This counsel have I found to tell,
Brought from my travels to my home : —
With staff and scallop do not crave
To see Christ's cradle and his grave.

Turn inward! there in clearest day
View Bethlehem and Golgotha.

O heart! what helps it, that the knee
Upon His natal spot is bended?
What helps it, reverently to see
The grave from which He soon ascended?
Let Him within thee find his birth;
And do thou die to things of earth,
And live Him; — let this be for aye
Thy Bethlehem and Golgotha.

THE EVENING SONG.

On a hill-side I stood,
As the sun was near its set;
And saw how o'er the wood
Hung Evening's golden net.

The cloud of heaven fell
  In dew upon Earth's calm breast;
At sound of the vesper bell
  All nature sunk to rest.

I said: "Now share, O heart,
  Creation's kind release;
Take, as its child, thy part,
  And lull thyself to peace.

"The flowers, with weary look,
  Their eyes are shutting slow,
And every running brook
  Is softened in its flow.

"The o'er-tired moth, close by,
  Under the leaf would creep;
In the sedge the dragon-fly
  Drops all bedewed asleep.

"The golden beetle makes
His cradle in the rose ;
The shepherd's flock now seeks
The fold for its repose.

"The skylark in the clover
Her damp nest stoops to find;
Beneath the forest cover
Lie down the hart and hind.

"If but a hut 's his own,
Man rests him there from pain ;
And though from it far and lone,
In dreams he 's back again.

"There seizes me a passion
Of longing and regret;
That I reach no such station, —
No home of the soul as yet.'

MIDNIGHT.

At still midnight
  I raise my sight
  To gaze upon the sky.
  No star of all on high
  Is shining bright,
  At still midnight.

At still midnight
  My thoughts invite
  A look into the dark.
  I see no cheerful spark
  Of mental light
  At still midnight.

At still midnight
  I do not slight

The measured beats of my heart ;
One single pulse of smart
Throbs full and tight
At still midnight.

At still midnight
I fight the fight
Of all thy woes, O man !
But settle it ne'er can,
With all my might,
At still midnight.

At still midnight
I yield up quite
To Thee the whole control,
O ruling Hand and Soul
Thou watchest right
At still midnight.

SICILIAN.

Lov'st thou for Beauty?
O love not me!
Love thou the Sun then;
His locks all gold appear.
Lov'st thou for Youth?
O love not me!
Love then the Spring,
That's youthful every year.
Lov'st thou for Riches?
O love not me!
Love the mermaiden,
With wealth of pearls so clear.
Lov'st thou for Love's sake?
O yes, love me!
Love me for ever,
To me for ever dear.

FROM

"LOVE'S SPRING."

I.

THY love o'er my life stole on,
As the breath of the Spring first blows ; —
When the Winter is scarce yet gone.
Earth heeds not how warm it grows.
But the Sun its sly power will shoot,
And reaches her heart e'en now ;
And the sap is astir at the root,
Long before it is seen in the bough.
The snow melts, the clouds pass away,
The bud of the year is begun ;
Then she stands in the full-glowing ray,
And wonders how all was done.

II.

O, LOVE is higher than what thou lovest ;
And though she may seem of Earth,

And be named however thou most approvest,
She is one, and of heavenly birth.
As when, under shifted masks' disguises,
In halls where the lamps burn bright,
One darling in many shapes tantalizes,
Till unveiled at last to sight; —
So loved I this, and then that, most dearly,
As the changing fancy might bid;
At last they were all masks merely,
Underneath which Love was hid.

III.

TELL me naught of Paradise;
'T is too large for me;
I have rather chosen this
Close felicity.
Tell me naught of Paradise;
'T is too far for me;
I have rather chosen this
Near felicity.

My beloved's bower, — O this
  Near felicity
Lies with all its Eden bliss
  Never too far to see!
My beloved's bower, — O this
  Close felicity
Holds for me nine paradises,
  That wide as heaven be!

FIVE LITTLE STORIES,

AS

LULLABIES FOR MY LITTLE SISTER.

FOR CHRISTMAS, 1813.

Once, Songs as Lullabies to thee I sung;
To sleep has sung thee now an angel's tongue.

But to awake above, art thou here fallen asleep;
Farewell! Thou art in Port, we on the stormy Deep.

St. John's Day, 1835.

I.

OF THE LITTLE BOY, THAT WISHED TO HAVE SOMEBODY CARRY HIM EVERYWHERE.

ONLY think! a little boy one day
Went out in the meadow grounds to stray;
But there he grew tired sore,
And said: "I can bear no more;
Would but something come near,
And take me from here!"

Now a little brook came flowing on,
And took up the little boy anon;
And on the brook he sits with joy;
"I am well off here," says the little boy.

But what 's the matter? The stream was cold,
And this full soon to his cost was told.
    It began to freeze him sore,
    And he said: "I can bear no more;
    Would but something come near,
    And take me from here!"

Then a little ship came sailing on,
And took up the little boy anon;
As in the ship he sits with joy,
"I am well off here," says the little boy.

But do you see? the vessel was small;
The little boy thinks, "I shall presently fall."
    He begins to tremble sore,
    And says: "I can bear no more;
    Would but something come near
    And take me from here!"

And now a snail comes creeping on,
And takes up the little boy anon;

In the snail's round house he sits with joy;
"I am well off here," says the little boy.

But think! the snail is no good steed,
And her steps were very slow indeed.
  He begins to fidget sore,
  And says: "I can bear no more;
  Would but something come near
  And take me from here!"

And behold! a horseman came galloping on,
And took up the little boy anon;
As behind the rider he sat with joy,
"I am well off here," said the little boy.

But look! like the wind he scoured along:
For the little boy it was quite too strong;
  He was bumped about, galled sore,
  And said: "I can bear no more;
  Would but something come near,
  And take me from here!"

At last, a tree that was standing there
Caught up the little boy by the hair ;
High he swings at the end of the bough,
And there the poor fellow is kicking now.

The child asks :
" Did the boy die then ? "
Answer :
" No ; he is kicking still !
To-morrow let's go and take him down."

II.

OF THE LITTLE TREE THAT WANTED TO HAVE OTHER LEAVES.

A LITTLE tree stood up in the wood,
  In bright and dirty weather;
And nothing but needles it had for leaves,
  From top to bottom together.
The needles stuck about,
And the little tree spoke out: —

"My companions all have leaves
  Beautiful to see,
While I've nothing but these needles; —
  No one touches me.
Might I have my fortune told,
All my leaves should be pure gold."

The little tree 's asleep by dark,
  Awake by earliest light;
And now its golden leaves you mark; —
  There was a sight!
The little tree says: "Now I 'm set high;
No tree in the wood has gold leaves but I."

But now again the night came back;
  Through the forest there walked a Jew,
With great thick beard and great thick sack,
  And soon the gold leaves did view.
He pockets them all, and away does fare,
Leaving the little tree quite bare.

The little tree speaks up distressed:
  "Those golden leaves how I lament!
I 'm quite ashamed before the rest,
  Such lovely dress to them is lent.
Might I bring one more wish to pass,
I would have my leaves of the clearest glass.'

The little tree sleeps again at dark,
  And wakes with the early light.
And now its glass leaves you may mark ; —
    There was a sight !
The little tree says : " Now I'm right glad,
No tree in the wood is so brightly clad."

There came up now a mighty blast,
  And a furious gale it blew ;
It swept among the trees full fast,
  And on the glass leaves it flew.
There lay the leaves of glass
All shivered on the grass.

The little tree complains :
  " My glass lies on the ground ;
Each other tree remains
  With its green dress all round.
Might I but have my wish once more,
I would have of those good green leaves good store."

Again asleep is the little tree,
  And early wakes to the light;
He is covered with green leaves fair to see,—
  He laughs outright;
And says : "I am now all nicely drest,
Nor need be ashamed before the rest."

And now, with udders full,
  Forth a wild she-goat sprung,
Seeking for herbs to pull,
  To feed her young.
She sees the leaves, nor makes much talk,
But strips all clear to the very stalk.

The little tree again is bare,
  And thus to himself he said:
"No longer for any leaves I care,
  Whether green, or yellow, or red.
If I had but my needles again,
I would never more scold or complain."

The little tree slept sad that night,
  And sadly opened his eye; —
He sees himself in the sun's first light,
  And laughs as he would die.
And all the trees in a roar burst out;
But the little tree little cared for their flout.

What made the little tree laugh like mad?
  And what set the rest in a roar?
In a single night soon back he had
  Every needle he had before.
And everybody may see them such;
Go out and look, — but do not touch.

Why not, I pray?
They prick, some say.

III.

OF THE LITTLE TREE THAT WENT TO TAKE A WALK.

A LITTLE tree there stood
In a pleasant shady wood,
Where many a shrub and bush
And more small trees did push;
Standing so thick along,
They made a real throng.

The little tree must need
Keep very close indeed.
So the little tree she thought, —
And made it clear she ought, —
"I'll here no longer stay,
But go elsewhere away,

And try some place to reach
Where 's neither birch nor beech,
Where 's neither oak nor fir,
Nor any the like of her.
By myself will I advance,
    And dance."

The little tree goes her ways,
And comes up to a place
Upon an open meadow,
Without a tree to shadow.
Here she stops advancing,
And has her dancing.

Whatever meets her sight
Does the little tree delight.
The sweetest little spring
Is close by murmuring,
Ready to cool her sweat
In Summer's glowing heat.

The beautiful sunlight
Is just as ready quite ;
If the little tree 's a-cold,
The sun warms up its mould.
And then a pleasant wind
Bears her a friendly mind,
And helps her with its breath,
While dancing on the heath.

The tree she danced and sprung
The entire Summer long ;
Till with jumping up and down
She has wholly lost her crown.
Her crown with its leaves so small, —
From her head she has dropped them all ;
On every side they 're strown,
And the little tree has none.
Some in the fountain lay,
And some in the sun's ray ;
The rest of all their kind
Were flying in the wind.

Cold is the Autumn's gale,
And the shivering tree grows pale.
And she cries to the spring below:
" Give me my leaves here now,
That in the Winter drear
I may have clothes to wear."
The fountain said: " No more
Can I the leaves restore;
I drank them all quite up,
They are sunk down in my cup."

She turned from the fount her cry,
And called to the sun on high:
" Give me my leaves back, you,
For I'm freezing through and through."
And the sun replied: " No more
Can I the leaves restore;
They crisped up long ago
Within my hot hands' glow."

Then the little tree in haste
Cried to the wind that passed :
" Give me my leaves again,
Or I sink upon the plain."
And the Wind replied : " No more
Can I the leaves restore.
Over the hills they 've flown,
Upon my swift wings blown."
Then the little tree spoke low :
" Now what I 'll do I know.
'T is too cold here to stay ;
I 'll to the wood away,
And under hedge and bough
Will find a screen somehow."

The little tree pauses not,
But sets off at a round trot ;
For the wood she scuds along,
To take place among the throng.
She asks the first tree there :

"Have you any room to spare?"
The answer is: "Not I."
Then another will she try.
But that again has none; —
So she goes to another one.
All round she makes her race,
But there 's not a single space.
Whilst it was pleasant Summer,
There was room for no new-comer;
Now, in the Winter weather,
They cuddled more together.
She found it all in vain; —
No foothold could she gain.

So on she sadly goes,
And cold, for she had no clothes;
And as off the poor thing packs,
There comes a man with an axe,
Rubbing his hands, and shaking,
As if with the cold he was aching.

Thinks quite bold the little tree:
"'T is a woodcutter, I see.
He 'll best cure me, if he will,
Of this dreadful, frosty chill."
To bring the thing to an end,
She cries to the woodman: "Friend,
It pinches thee as me;
It pinches me as thee;
Thou canst be help of mine;
I can be help of thine.
Come, cut me down,
And take me to town;
And kindle a fire,
That I can raise higher;
So thou warmest me,
And I thee."

The woodcutter thought the plan not bad,
And quick to his axe recourse he had.
At the root the axe he plies,

And root and branch soon down she lies.
And he saws, and he splits,
And he carries home the bits ;
And now and then a billet
Puts under pot or skillet.

The largest stick of all
Happens our way to fall.
The cook its chips shall bring,
And on the embers fling ;
And for a week entire
They 'll make for our soup the fire.

Porridge ! you say.
Well, have your way.

IV.

THE MUSICIAN.

THE player tunes his kit;
To it says he:
"Thou must show thy skill a bit;
Come, go with me."
Before a castle he goes to play;
'Tis night, and the player fiddles away.
The player says: "I will not give o'er;
I must still fiddle one stroke more."

Before the castle a garden lies,
With trees and plants.
They must have seen with some surprise
Their time to dance.
The player before the castle will play,
And the trees set out to dance away.

The player says: "I will not give o'er;
I must still fiddle one stroke more."

The garden doth contain a lake,
And fish within;
And they too hear the fiddle's shake,
And to frisk begin.
The player before the castle will play,
And the trees and the fishes caper away.
The player says: "I will not give o'er;
I must still fiddle one stroke more."

Within the castle there are some mice;
He fiddles yet;
And the little fellows hear in a trice,
And up they get.
The player before the castle will play;
Trees, fishes, and mice are dancing away.
The player says: "I will not give o'er;
I must still fiddle one stroke more."

Within the castle are bench and table;
They 're waking up;
They hobble along as well as they 're able,
And join the troop.
The player before the castle will play;
Trees, fish, mice, benches, are dancing away.
The player says: "I will not give o'er;
I must still fiddle one stroke more."

"Are there, then, here no men at all?"
The player cries;
"I am playing to nothing but the bare wall;
They don't open their eyes.
Trees, fish, mice, benches, are dancing free;
Will they not come out of their castle to me?"
The player says: "I will not give o'er;
I must still fiddle one stroke more."

The castle at that begins to feel
Alive;

And all on end to that wild reel
Will drive.
The player fiddles, the castle jumps,
But the men sleep on, nor will stir their stumps.
The player says: "I will not give o'er;
I must still fiddle one stroke more."

And the castle jumps till it flies apart
With a crack;
And the men in bed at last hear, and start,
And wake.
They hear the musician at his play,
And dance with the rest, as brisk as they.
The player says: "I will now give o'er;—
Yet still will I fiddle one stroke more."

And why so?
For the little man in the goose.
And must he dance as loose?
You 'll soon know.

V.

THE LITTLE MAN IN THE GOOSE.

THE little man went out to walk one day
    Upon the roof. Take care!
The roof is narrow, the little man gay; —
    He 'll surely fall off there.
Before he thinks, down he comes by a blunder,
But breaks not his neck, and that is a wonder.

Under the roof stood a washing-tub;
    There he soused out of sight.
It will take to dry him many a rub; —
    Ah! served him right.
Now the goose comes running up,
And swallows the little man at a sup.

The goose has gobbled the mannikin,
For her stomach was large to hold;
But the mannikin pinched her well within,
That must be told.
The goose sets up great lamentation,
And causes the cook-maid great vexation.

Cook takes to her knife the whetter,
For else it would not cut:
" This goose cries so, we had better
Bring it across her throat.
We 'll kill her, I believe,
For a roast on Christmas Eve."

The goose is plucked and drawn by the cook,
And roast;
But the little man dared not take a look,
Thou know'st.
The goose was really cooked to a charm;
And what after this can the little man harm?

On Christmas Eve comes to table the goose
In a pannikin.
The father carves for present use.
— And the mannikin? —
When the goose was fairly divided,
The little man creep out at the side did.

The father springs from the table apace, —
Leaves his empty chair afar; —
The little man, quietly taking his place,
Carries into the goose the war.
Quoth he: "You have me devoured;
Now here 's for you, you coward."

So the little man eats with an appetite,
As if he alone were seven;
And we all fall on, as if in spite,
To be with the little man even;
Till nothing is left of the goose but his mittens,
And they shall be left for the sport of the kittens.

The mouse nothing won,
And the story is done.

" What 's all you 've said, I pray ? "
" Jests for Christmas holiday ;
At New Year thou learnest — "
" Well, say ! "
" To be in earnest."

1835.

Early wert thou into the school of days
Sent, and hast through it passed, and gained thy praise.

Young, — but each trial hast thou so withstood,
Thou art now called out, for further progress good.

High mind, but never proud! Low heart, but never mean!
Those prizes bright on thy pure breast were seen.

Long after us thou hast the course begun;
But, all unlooked for, now the start hast won.

The height is reached thou early wouldst attain,
While we on these low forms must still remain.

A sign that we not yet enough have learned,
To join those classes where thy praise was earned.

UHLAND.

KING CHARLES'S VOYAGE.

KING CHARLES, with his twelve peers so brave,
For Holy Land was bound;
The bark was pitching on the wave,
The storm was raging round.

Then spoke the eager knight Roland:
"I can both fend and hit;
But winds and billows to withstand,
This art is poorly fit."

And spoke Sir Holgar, — he the Dane:
 "I skill to play the harp;
But what boots that? 'T is all in vain,
 When blast and surge drive sharp."

He eyed his steel with saddened air,
 The brave Sir Olivier:
"It is not for myself I care
 As for the Altaclear." *

These words the subtle Ganelon
 Half smothered in his breast:
"Were some way out to *me* but shown,
 The Devil might take the rest."

---

* The heroes of romance were accustomed to give names to their swords. That of Rinaldo was Fusberta. Every reader of Ariosto is familiar with the Durindana of Orlando, or Roland. Sir Otuel laid about him with Corrouge. King Arthur's magic blade was Escalibore. Sir Bevis of Southampton rejoiced in his Morglay. Charlemagne called his sword "La Joyeuse." — TRANSLATOR.

Archbishop Turpin sorely sighed :
  " O sinful men are we !
Come, dearest Saviour, o'er the tide,
  And lead us safe and free."

Count Richard up, and undismayed :
  " Ye spirits damned from hell !
Many 's the service to you I 've paid ; —
  Now turn and serve me well."

Then spoke Sir Naimis : " Many a wight
  I 've counselled well and clear ;
But good sweet water, and counsel bright,
  At sea are rather dear."

Said Sir Riòl, with locks all gray :
  " An old sword-blade am I,
And frankly would my body lay
  At last in ground that 's dry."

It was Sir Guy, a gentle knight,
Who thus began to sing :
" O if I were a bird, my flight
Swift to my love I'd wing !"

Out spoke the noble Count Garein :
" God help us now, and keep !
Much rather would I drink red wine,
Than water from the deep."

Sir Lambert cried, a gay gallant :
" Let Heaven still helpful be !
I 'd rather eat a good fish, I grant,
Than have the fish eat me."

Sir Godfrey, that great Paladin,
Said : " Come what may befall !
No other lot will for me have been,
Than for my brothers all."

King Charles at the helm sat firm and still ; —
    No word he turned to say ; —
But steered with constant hand and will,
    Till the storm had lulled away.

BARON VON ZEDLITZ.

THE NIGHT REVIEW.

At midnight hour the drummer
Gets up from his grave so low;
With his drum his round he marches,
Goes briskly to and fro.

With his fleshless arms the drumsticks
He plies in measure true;
Strikes many a rapid roll-call,
Reveillé and tattoo.

The drum sounds strange and ghostly,
It has a mighty beat;
The slain and mouldering soldiers
Rise at it on their feet.

And they in frosts of Russia,
All stiff with ice and storm;
And they that lie in Italy,
Where they find the earth too warm;

They whom the Nile mud covers,
And the Arabian sand,
They stalk out from their charnels,
And muskets take in hand.

* * * *

At midnight hour the cornet
Gets up from his grave so low;
He peals into his trumpet,
And rides forth to and fro.

Then on their airy horses
Come the dead riders old,
The bloody veteran squadrons,
With weapons manifold.

The whitened skulls are grinning,
Beneath the helms they wear ;
And skeleton the fingers
That the long sabres bear.

* * * *

At midnight hour the chieftain
Gets up from his grave so low ;
By all his staff attended,
He comes forth riding slow.

He wears a little hat,
And a coat quite plain has on,
And slender is the sword
That at his side hangs down.

The morn with yellow lustre
O'er all the broad field shines;
The man with the little hat
Looks down along the lines.

The ranks present their muskets, —
Then shoulder, — then away,
With drum and clarion sounding,
Sweeps on the whole array.

The generals and marshals
Stand round in circle near;
The chief speaks to the nearest
One low word in his ear.

The word goes round that circle,
Then echoes far and wide;
"France!" is the watchword given, —
"St. Helena!" replied.

This is the grand parade
In the Elysian field,
That, as twelve o'clock is striking,
Is by dead Cæsar held.

COUNT VON AUERSPERG,

UNDER THE NAME OF

ANASTASIUS GRÜN.

THE LAST POET.

"When will you bards be weary
    Of rhyming on? How long
Ere it is sung and ended,
    The old eternal song?

"Is it not long since empty, —
    The horn of full supply;
And all the posies gathered,
    And all the fountains dry?"

As long as the Sun's chariot
  Shall keep its azure track,
And but one human visage
  Give answering glances back;

As long as skies shall nourish
  The thunderbolt and gale,
And, frightened at their fury,
  One throbbing heart shall quail;

As long as after tempest
  Shall spring one showery bow,
One breast with peaceful promise
  Of reconcilement glow;

As long as Night the concave
  Sows with her starry seed,
And but one man those letters
  Of golden writ can read;

Long as a moonbeam glimmers,
　　Or bosom sighs a vow ;
Long as the wood-leaves rustle,
　　To cool a weary brow ;

As long as roses blossom,
　　And earth is green in May ;
As long as eyes shall sparkle
　　And smile in Pleasure's ray ;

As long as cypress-shadows
　　The graves more mournful make,
Or one cheek 's wet with weeping,
　　Or one poor heart can break ; —

So long on earth shall wander
　　The Goddess Poesy ;
And with her one, exulting
　　Her votarist to be.

And singing on, triumph'ing,
The old earth-mansion through,
Out marches the last minstrel ; —
He is the last man too.

The Lord holds the creation
Forth in his hand meanwhile,
Like a fresh flower just opened,
And views it with a smile.

When once this Flower-Giant
Begins to show decay,
And earths and suns are flying
Like blossom-dust away, —

Then ask, — if of the question
Not weary yet, — how long
Ere it is sung and ended,
The old eternal song!

MEN'S TEARS

MAIDEN, didst thou see me weeping ? —
　　Ah ! methinks that woman's tear
Is like the soft dew out of heaven,
　　That in the flower-cup glitters clear.

If the troubled Night hath wept it,
　　Or the smiling Morning shed,
Still the dew the flower refreshes,
　　And renewed it lifts its head.

But the tear of man resembles
　　Precious gum from Eastern tree ;
In the very heart deep hidden,
　　Seldom starting quick and free.

Through the bark thou must cut sharply,
To the pith the steel must go;
Then the pure and noble moisture,
Bright and golden, trickles slow.

Soon, indeed, is dried its fountain,
And the tree fresh foliage gains,
And yet shall welcome many a Summer;
But the cut, the scar, remains.

Maiden, think of that tree wounded,
Where its growths the Orient rears;
Maiden, of that man bethink thee
Whom thine eyes have seen in tears.

ORIGINAL PIECES.

HYMNS.

I.

FOR THE ORDINATION OF MR. WILLIAM P. LUNT, AT NEW YORK, JUNE 19, 1828.

O God, whose presence glows in all
  Within, around us, and above;
Thy Word we bless, thy Name we call,
  Whose Word is Truth, whose Name is Love.

That Truth be with the heart believed
  Of all who seek this sacred place!
With power proclaimed, in peace received,
  Our spirit's light, thy Spirit's grace!

That Love its holy influence pour,
To keep us meek, and make us free,
And throw its binding blessing more
Round each with all, and all with Thee!

Direct and guard the youthful strength
Devoted to thy Son this day ;
And give thy word full course at length
O'er man's defects and time's decay.

Send down its angel to our side!
Send in its calm upon the breast!
For we would know no other guide
And we can need no other rest.

II.

FOR THE INSTALLATION OF REV. WILLIAM P. LUNT, AT QUINCY, MASS., JUNE 3, 1835.*

WE meditate the day
Of triumph and of rest,
When, shown of God and shaped in clay,
The Word was manifest.

The angels saw and sung;
Earth listened far and wide;
Believed and preached, — a faith, a tongue, —
The Word was glorified.

Lord! give it gracious sweep,
And here its errand bless,
Whose mercy sent it o'er the deep,
To glad the wilderness.

* The sermon was on the manifestation of Christ.

Shoot forth its starry * light
To guide our pilgrim way ;
A sign of hope through this world's night,
And brighter than its day.

Again thy witness-voice !
Again thy Spirit-Dove ! *
That hearts may in its trust rejoice,
And soften with its love.

Send round its blessed cup,*
As once in Galilee ;
And catch our dull affections up
To heaven, and Christ, and Thee.

---

* One of three ancient symbols in the Church of Christ's manifestation to the Gentiles.

III.

FOR THE ORDINATION OF MR. HENRY W. BELLOWS, AT NEW YORK, 1839.

O LORD of life, and truth, and grace,
Ere nature was begun!
Make welcome to our erring race
Thy Spirit and thy Son.

We hail the Church, built high o'er all
The heathens' rage and scoff;
Thy providence its fenced wall,
"The Lamb the light thereof."

Thy Christ hath reached his heavenly seat
Through sorrows and through scars;
The golden lamps are at his feet,
And in his hand the stars.*

---

* Rev. ii. 1.

O, may he walk among us here,
With his rebuke and love, —
A brightness o'er this lower sphere,
A ray from worlds above!

Teach thou thy youthful servant, Lord!
The mysteries he reveals,
That reverence may receive the word,
And meekness loose the seals.

IV.

FOR THE CENTENNIAL CELEBRATION OF THE ALUMNI OF HARVARD COLLEGE, AUGUST 23, 1842.

The hands of twice a hundred years
Point each one to its Class; —
Their eyes behold, through joy and tears,
Each brief procession pass.

We praise the Immortal Providence,
That early watched and late;
That kindled light, and spread defence,
And made the small one great.

We bless this Fountain's earliest rill
Of piety and lore;
We bless the streams that gladden still
The land they fed before.

With joy we greet this throng of sons,
As to a Mother led;
And think of all our noble ones,—
The absent and the dead.

Look on us, Lord! before whose sight
The ages are a day;
Reveal to us thy tokens bright,
And cheer with steady ray.

Thy blessing meet this gathered band,
Its aged and its youth!
Be Worth and Wisdom on each hand,
And overhead the TRUTH.

Thy blessing guide the lengthening line,
That hence shall fruitful run!
The fruit be as of Sorek's vine;
The line as of the Sun!

V.

FOR THE ORDINATION OF MR. RUFUS ELLIS, AT NORTHAMPTON, JUNE 7, 1843.

THINE, Lord, these heavens on high,
And thine this earth around;
Thy goodness travels through the sky,
And blossoms from the ground.

Thine too the human soul,
    With heights and breadths unknown ;
The rays and drops at thy control,
    And seed and sod thine own.

But man must watch and toil
    For fruits that thrive below ;
And dress and keep that dearer soil
    Whence life or death shall grow.

Sow here the Gospel Word,
    And heavenly influence send,
And teach us all as servants, Lord,
    To labor and depend.

An earnest purpose grant,
    And give the work success;
And O, may Grace and Duty plant
    A field that Thou wilt bless !

VI.

FOR THE DEDICATION OF THE NEW HOUSE OF WORSHIP BUILT BY THE PROPRIETORS OF THE SECOND CHURCH IN BOSTON, SEPTEMBER 17, 1845.

THY way is in unbounded space,
In air, and earth, and sea;—
Thy way is in the Holy Place
That man doth build to Thee.

The soul thy temple is, O Lord,
And thy true service pays;—
Yet here dost Thou thy name record,
And here accept our praise.

To us, as to thy prophet, deign
To speak thy word and will;
And let the glory of thy train
This house of worship fill.

The vision on his eye that broke
    Here pour upon the soul; —
Thy people's prayer the censer's smoke,
    Thy love the altar's coal.

And when to Thee they humbly cry,
    Or gratefully confess,
O hear them in thy dwelling high,
    And when Thou hearest, bless!

VII.

FOR THE INSTALLATION OF REV. DAVID FOSDICK, AS MINISTER OF THE HOLLIS STREET SOCIETY, BOSTON, MARCH 3, 1846.

The patriarch's dove, on weary wing,
    One leaf of olive found,
Within the narrow ark to bring,
    When all the earth was drowned.

The dove of God, in happier hour,
    O'er Jordan's sweeter wave,
In symbol showed the Spirit's power,
    That all the earth would save.

O Lord! to this our sacred rite
    Such gracious tokens grant,
As make thy temples, where they light,
    Thine Arks of Covenant.

And still on Life's baptizing tide,
    Or Sorrow's bitter sea,
Decending Peace be multiplied,
    And hallow hearts to Thee!

VIII.

FOR THE ORDINATION OF MR. O. B. FROTHINGHAM, AS MINISTER OF THE NORTH CHURCH IN SALEM, MARCH 10, 1847.

A PSALM.

"The Lord gave the word"; 't was the word of his Truth,
And the word of Salvation for all men to be.
Then forth went its preachers, — the aged, the youth,
And "great was the company."

"The Lord gave the word"; it was not as of old,
When the Ark of his Strength to the Temple was brought;
'Mid the clanging of steel, and the gleaming of gold,
And spoils of a battle fought.

But the Gospel of Faith in the Spirit of Love
Is the true "King of Glory" the Church has enshrined;
And "the chariots of God" are the "thousands" that move
As angels to bless mankind.

O Lord, give this word its triumphant success!
Be its mercy and peace on thy worshippers here!
And clothe thy young priest with its righteousness,
With its earnest joy and fear.

IX.

FOR THE DEDICATION OF THE CHURCH OF THE SAVIOUR, BOSTON, NOVEMBER 10, 1847.

O Saviour! whose immortal Word
For ever lasts the same;
Thy grace within the walls afford,
Here builded to thy name.

No other name is named below,
  No other sign unfurled,
To lead our hope, or quell our woe,
  Or sanctify the world.

Here, many-tongued thy truth be found,
  And mind and heart employ;
Thy Law and Promise pour around
  Their terror and their joy!

Here may thy saints new progress make;
  Thy loitering ones be sped;
And here thy mourners comfort take,
  And here thy poor be fed!

May God, thy God, his Spirit send, —
  The word is else unblest, —
And fill this place from end to end,
  O Ark of strength and rest!

X.

FOR THE THIRTY-SECOND ANNUAL VISITATION OF THE DIVINITY SCHOOL AT CAMBRIDGE, JULY 14, 1848.

"Pray ye, therefore, the Lord of the harvest, that he will send forth laborers."

"Ye shall receive power, after that the Holy Ghost is come upon you."

WE hear the heavenly voice,
That bids us forward move;
And make its call our choice,
Our labor and our love.
White fields demand
The reaper's pains;
And dark-brown plains
The sower's hand.

The sickle and the seed
Still own one Sovereign Lord;

He gives the means we need,
And we but plant his word.
The laborer's skill,
And sun and rain,
And store of grain,
Abide his will.

Go with us, Lord, we pray!
Or we are left alone, —
Poor wanderers from thy way,
And aliens in our own.
The humble heart,
The fervid soul,
And faith all whole,
O God! impart.

Make this our Pentecost, —
Our day of tongues and fire!
With gifts we need the most,
Our languid minds inspire

O bless the hour,
And crown the end!
The Spirit send,
And then the Power.

XI.

FOR THE FIFTIETH ANNIVERSARY OF THE BOSTON FEMALE ASYLUM, SEPTEMBER 20, 1850.

THE grand Sabbatic year,
The Hebrew Jubilee,
With blast of trump and shout of cheer
Set slave and debtor free.

O how the dispossessed
Long languished for the sign!
How joyed at last to see that best,
That fiftieth cycle shine!

But no such lingering ray
    THIS charity awaits ;
For every year and every day
    It opens wide its gates.

It does not loose, but hold ;
    It says not, Go, — but, Come ;
And pens the feeblest in its fold,
    And builds the orphan's home.

O thanks for fifty years
    Of woman's pity shown!
For all it saved of Misery's tears,
    And Ruin's heavier moan !

Shield Thou her fatherless,
    O Father! we implore;
And make her efforts strong to bless
    For years and ages more.

XII.

FOR THE INSTALLATION OF REV. RUFUS ELLIS AS PASTOR OF THE FIRST CHURCH OF CHRIST IN BOSTON, MAY 4, 1853.

ETERNAL Lord! to Thee the church
Where now we praise and pray,
Though old to our historic search,
Is but of yesterday.

Of yesterday is all our race
To thine all-present sight;
Before thy Truth both Time and Place
Dissolve in higher light.

Yet here, O Heavenly Father, grant
Thy special Presence down!
Our fathers' God, the children's want
With chosen bounties crown!

O deign to write thy love and fear
Upon these humble walls,
And speak when sinful man shall hear,
And listen when he calls!

Train up this flock, a church indeed,
Unspotted, unenticed,
On thy dear Word of Life to feed,
And follow after Christ.

With light and strength, O Fount Divine!
Fill high thy servant's heart,
Who seeks anew the anointing sign, —
The grace thou shalt impart.

XIII.

COMMUNION HYMN.

"And he took bread, and gave thanks."

The Son of God gave thanks,
Before the bread he broke.
How high that calm devotion ranks
Among the words he spoke!

Thanks, 'mid those troubled men;
Thanks, in that dismal hour;
The world's dark prince advancing then
In all his rage and power.

Thanks, o'er that loaf's dread sign;
Thanks, o'er that bitter food;
And o'er the cup, that was not wine,
But sorrow, fear, and blood.

And shall our griefs resent
    What God appoints as best
When he, in all things innocent,
    Was yet in all distressed?

Shall we unthankful be
    For all our blessings round,
When in that press of agony
    Such room for thanks he found?

O shame us, Lord!—whate'er
    The fortunes of our days,—
If, suffering, we are weak to bear,
    If, favored, slow to praise.

XIV.

COMMUNION HYMN.

"Do this in remembrance of me."
"How he was known of them in breaking of bread."

"Remember me," the Saviour said,
On that forsaken night,
When from his side the nearest fled,
And death was close in sight.

Through all the following ages' track
The world remembers yet;
With love and worship gazes back,
And never can forget.

But who of us has seen his face,
Or heard the words he said?
And none can now his look retrace
In breaking of the bread.

O blest are they, who have not seen,
And yet believe him still!
They know him, when his praise they mean,
And when they do his will.

We hear his word along our way;
We see his light above;
Remember when we strive and pray,
Remember when we love.

XV.

FOR THE DEDICATION OF A UNITARIAN CHURCH.

One God, the Father, own;
Accept the Christ he gave;
Attend his Spirit, breathing down,
To teach, console, and save.

The Scripture thus we read;
 And bless its sacred plan,
To mould thy heart, and train thy creed,
 O wayward child of man!

Its essence, not its writ,
 Our guide and rule we call;
Not fastening down all Truth to It,
 But widening It to all.

With this free reverence, Lord,
 In covenant church estate,
In faith and brotherly accord,
 This house we dedicate.

Thy presence, Father, make
 Its refuge and supply!
For Truth and for thy Mercy's sake,
 Build up and sanctify.

Enlarge its sacred tent,
  Where earnest hearts shall meet,
And, rich with gracious gifts, be sent
  The inspiring Paraclete.

FRAGMENTS AND MEMORIES

FROM THE EARLY TIME.

LINES

WRITTEN IN THE CASE OF A WATCH, THE GIFT OF ——.

These slender wheels, by human skill combined,
But play their hours, and then forget to move.
Not so the motions of the immortal mind,
That runs in gratitude and beats with love.
No length of days, no varied scenes of life,
Shall make me heedless of my debts to thee.
In pleasure's calm, in sorrow's gloomiest strife,
I will be mindful, till I cease to be,
Of all that thou hast thought and wished and
done for me.

TO A SIGH.

I am not ill, I am not grieved,
Pain has not wrung, nor hope deceived;
Why, then, thou sad, unmeaning guest,
Disturb the comforts of my breast?

Is it because so slight a bound
'Twixt joy's extreme and grief is found,
That tears so oft dim rapture's eyes,
And bliss and anguish speak in sighs?

Meek child of wants, I know thee now;
A faithful monitor art thou,
To check Joy's rash, impetuous car,
And show how vain her triumphs are.

Then welcome, gentle stranger! Still
Refine my pleasures; tame my will;

Teach my uplifted heart to flee
From what is now to what shall be.
Thou dost but point me to a higher sphere,
For what wise Heaven denies us now and here.

THE RENUNCIATION.

Sweet visions of Fancy, deceitful as fair,
Though often misguiding, not cherished the less,
How oft have you solaced the moments of care,
And diffused your bright beams o'er the gloom of
distress!

How often has time flitted rapidly by,
When allured by your promise, or charmed by
your spell!

How often, when sad, though I could not tell why,
Have ye smiled that I loved your illusions so well!

Such have been my feelings, such has been your power;
Farewell! and oh! with you for ever adieu
All the flatteries that gilded my heart's dearest hour,
And the fervors that fancied those flatteries were true!

Farewell! At stern Duty's command I resign
All that once was so fondly, so foolishly dear.
Farewell! Though your transports no longer are mine,
I am freed from your longing, your terror, your tear.

O, no more may my spirit recline on your aid
Its sorrows to soothe, or its fears to disarm!

For the tints of the rainbows that flush but to
fade,
May I look to the white beams that lend them
their charm.

A SUMMER EVENING.

It is a lovely eve. Meek Twilight now
Begins her gentle, but too short-lived, reign.
The evening star glows in her radiant brow;
The painted clouds, slow rising from the west,
Her robes of state; her golden sandals press
The verge of heaven. It is a lovely eve.
How different from the morn, so lately seen!
Then all was life, and joy, and melody.
The sportive birds sang to the rising dawn,
And to the quickened sense the perfumed air

Seemed doubly fragrant, while the dewy grass
Glittered like Fancy's fairy-work ; — the sun
Looked on it longer, and the tints so brave
Like the gay dreams of youth dissolved in air.
Now all is calm and still. No more the groves
Echo the songsters' cheerful, various music.
Naught breaks the silence but the frog's rude croak
Discordant, jarring from the distant pool.
Yet say, is not such contemplative hour,
When all around breathes peace, more dear to thee
Than all the transient splendors of the morn?

But see! the sun, long sunk beneath the west,
Spreads his last glories o'er the evening cloud.
How many eyes, that mark his setting ray,
Shall never see his rising! Even so,
Father! for so it seemeth good to Thee.
The longest day that man must dwell on earth,
How short, how doubtful! Yet in this brief space
We toil, and strive, and sigh, and are content.

The twilight now has closed ; but all the scene
Of wonders is not ended. Crowning all,
The mystic Night, with all her train of worlds,
Appears sublime in beauty. Fancy now
Escapes from earth, and soars beyond the stars.
Dear sister, so let our short day be spent,
That, when our sun is set, its parting beams
May shine on years yet distant; and when Time
Has whelmed us in the wreck of all that 's gone,
Our rising may be joyous!

TO ——, BEREFT OF REASON.

O Lady! still in Memory's dream
Restored to all thou wast I seem,
And weep, each image to redeem
Of days so fair,

Nor dare recall the poor, quenched beam,
That once shone there.

Where now that gem of thought and feeling,
The changeful light of the soul revealing, —
Thy glance, — to every heart appealing?
Its play is o'er;
And that warm smile of witchery's stealing
Will charm no more.

Let me not think how swift the day,
Of peace and rapture sped away,
When thou wouldst listen to my lay,
And crown the while
Thine own bard with his chosen bay,
Affection's smile.

That time is past; long hushed that strain,
Which never can be waked again;
Thou heed'st not now; and I in vain

A mute form deck;
Yet ever near my heart remain,
Thou lovely wreck!

Long, vacant months 'tis thine to know,
Where neither joys nor griefs can grow;
Chilled is thy spirit's fervid flow,
And hope is none.
O beam from that blank waste of snow
Thy look, — but one!

The land of light and God's own grace
Shall re-illume thy mindless face.
No soul's eclipse to reach that place!
No griefs to tell!
Till then, my hand can only trace,
Farewell! Farewell!

TO ——.

You tell me I 'm sad; — that my spirit appears
As if worn by the traces of time and of tears;
Though few summers yet have flown over my head,
And many and bright are the blessings they shed.
You tell me I 'm changed; and that joy's sunny ray
Which once kindled within me has quite sunk away;
And you ask if regret, or misfortune, or care,
Has dimmed the gay sparkles that once sported there.

O, if e'er was a spot on this tempest-torn world,
Where no blight has consumed, and no storm-bolt been hurled;
Where Nature 's all smiles, and earth loves to entwine

Its best selfish pleasures, — that spot has been
mine.
Ambition scarce planned more than effort achieved,
And Hope always promising never deceived.
Friends dear as existence have ever stood round
me;
Success, that should humble each vain thought,
has crowned me;
And do not believe that there throbs in this breast
A heart, that can cheerless and thankless be blest.
Do you ask, Why, then, pensive, thus circled with
bliss?
Can you ask, in a world frail and changing like
this?
Perhaps there 's a charm in this sad hue of thought
More pleasing than all that gay moments have
brought;
Or perhaps some high passion has calmed my
wild breast,
As the thunder at sea lulls the surges to rest.

Perhaps, too intent on the future, I gaze
O'er the dim, doubtful forms of the far-distant
 days;
Or perhaps some new changes of feeling and scene
Call to mournful remembrance the days that have
 been;
And there crowd on the heart thoughts of long-
 perished ill,
And of sorrows that speak not, but linger there
 still.
Or perhaps 't is the world's sins and follies I moan,
As I blame others' failings, and sigh for my own.
O, who has not trembled at wrong's wide-spread
 reign,
And blushed to have shared in its woe and its
 stain?

Far, far be the day, when thy young heart shall
 know
Of affections pierced through, and of loved ones
 brought low;

Of the weakness, unkindness, and arts of man-
kind, —
The deceits that allure, and the passions that
blind!
Heaven long shield from sorrow that spirited brow,
And the world's trials leave you e'en purer than
now!
Full sweet are the flowers that around you are
blowing,
And bright are the streams that around you are
flowing;
But ill may their brightness and sweetness com-
pare
With the light-hearted thoughts that go wander-
ing there;
And rich as the view is of tree, brook, and hill,
Life's first opening prospects are lovelier still.
Rejoice in the vision! nor think, merry maid,
How the flowers will droop, and the scenery fade.

TO A. G. F.

AT SEA.

I THOUGHT of you in my lonely hours,
While watching the clouds, the stars, the deep;
Or tasking my mind's intentest powers,
Or courting the visions of welcome sleep.
I thought of you when the laugh went round
At the deck and cabin's boisterous cheer;
No voice that I loved was in the sound,
And their foreign speech disturbed my ear.

I thought of you, when the winds have slept,
And the ship scarce rocked on the lazy sea.

How heavily on the long hours swept
In waveless and dull monotony !
I thought of you, when the clouds heaved dark,
And the furthermost swell in foam was curled.
She sees not, I said, our plunging bark,
She hears not the din of this watery world.

I thought of you, when the morn's young ray
Tinged the ocean mists and the ocean foam ;
And I prayed it might bring a happy day
To the friends I have left, and my far-off home.
I thought of you, when the glorious sun
Went down behind the deep, round sea.
He had hours of light yet left for one,
Who is dear as his blessed beams to me.

My course to other climes I bend ;
My tongue to other accents frame ;
My gaze to other scenes extend ;
But still my heart, the same, the same,
Turns back to you.

A SUNSET IN ITALY.

WHENCE do the Spirits of the Air
Breathe gentlest, kindliest?
When their wind-harps and balm they bear
From their chambers in THE WEST.

When glow the many-colored skies
In their richest beauty drest?
When the sunset flings its gorgeous dies
O'er its curtains in THE WEST.

Like that soft air to a weary brow,
And the throbs of an anxious breast,
Come thoughts of the dear and distant now
From the home that's in THE WEST.

Like those fair skies, where to fancy's sight
　　Float forms as of spirits blest,
Seems the golden gleam of each dear delight,
　　That dwells there in THE WEST.

O land, of all that bright orb gilds
　　The freest, happiest, best!
Take me back from the pomp of these blushing fields
　　To thy proud shores in THE WEST.

O more than all, my own loved one!
　　When shall the wanderer rest,
And watch with you that sinking sun
　　Far deeper down THE WEST?

TO A CHANGING FRIEND.

—◆—

I.

Thy leaves are rustling to my tread,
    Thou falling Year!
Once by the showers and sunbeams fed,
    Now dry and sear;
Once waving gay above my head,
    Now scattered here.
So fallen, and trampled on, and dead,
    The joys appear
Of parting Friendship, fancy-led,
    But pure as dear.
To memory of that dream all fled,
    This tomb I rear;

And o er that page of life, all read,
Just drop this tear.
Farewell! — The bitter word I 've said,
Nor wish, nor fear.

II.

It is not when the pulse is gone,
For ever closed the eye,
And breath in the cold form is none,
Men die.

'T is when all hope resigns its breath, —
The eye no help can see, —
The pulse beats downward, — that seems death
To me.

So, when Affection shows decay,
    And warmth and cheer are fled,
The heart already lays away
        Its dead.

III.

Nay, break it off; why wear we
    The loosened tie, the same
As when the soul was in it,
    And it was not all a name?

It is as if the torn leaves,
    All trampled in the wet,
Should think to climb their branches,
    And make it Summer yet.

O, worse than sad! 'T is mockery,
That jeers us for the past,
And flouts with hollowest shadows
A joy too bright to last.

It tells of foolish dreaming,
And throbs of younger blood;
And ah! how we can ruin
An undecaying good.

I never can forget thee;
I never will upbraid;
And thou, — unsay not ever
The softest thou hast said.

'T were better far not meeting,
Than to meet in such a mind;
Then turn we from each other,
Ere cold thoughts grow unkind.

I 'll picture in my memory
    Thy loving looks of yore ;
And bless thee as I then did,
    But see thee never more.

SCATTERED.

THE BURYING-GROUND AT NEW HAVEN.

O, WHERE are they whose all that earth could
give
Beneath these senseless marbles disappeared?
Where even they who taught these stones to
grieve, —
The hands that hewed them, and the hearts
that reared?
Such the poor bounds of all that's hoped or
feared
Within the griefs and smiles of this short day.

Here sank the honored, vanished the endeared.
This the last tribute love to love could pay, —
An idle pageant-pile to graces passed away.

Why deck these sculptured trophies of the tomb?
Why, victims, garland thus the spoiler's fane ?
Hope ye by these to avert oblivion's doom,
In grief ambitious, and in ashes vain ?
Go, rather bid the sand the trace retain
Of all that parted Virtue felt and did !
Yet powerless man revolts from Ruin's reign ;
And Pride has gleamed upon the coffin-lid,
And heaped o'er human dust the mountain Pyramid.

Sink, mean memorials of what cannot die !
Be lowly as the relics you o'erspread !
Nor lift your funeral forms so gorgeously,
To tell who slumbers in each lowly bed.
I would not honor thus the sainted dead,

Nor to each stranger's careless eye declare
My sacred griefs for Joy and Friendship fled.
No, let me hide the names of those that were,
Deep in my stricken heart, and shrine them only
there.

IN AN ALBUM.

As bright a fortune wait thee, Mary,
As warms young hearts in tales of faery,
As kindles poet's sweetest themes,
As blesses maiden's dearest dreams!
Some Genius of the Enchanted Ring
All perils ward, all favors bring!
The Spirits of Earth, the Spirits of Air,
And of each kind influence gathered there,
Be waiting about thee from hour to hour

As queen of some charm of mystical power,
To lay at thy feet life's sparkling treasures,
And crown thy brows with its rosiest pleasures!

Such be the wish of some idle line!
A better wish for thee, maid, is mine.

May thine be as much of fortune's share,
As thou 'st worth to merit, and grace to wear,
And heart to improve, and strength to bear!
The beauty be thine that lasts for aye,
Though from feature and form it must pass away!
The Genius of Duty guard thy head,
When that of Romance shall be weak or dead!
Good thoughts and thine own heart's purity
Be the Spirits that ever wait on thee;
And for magical amulet or stone,
Be the trust that is fixed on Heaven alone!

SHAKESPEARE'S MULBERRY-TREE.

'T is sweet a deathless memory
With living things to bind;
With Nature's humblest turf or tree
Her mightiest Poet's mind.

The plant, beloved of that poor worm,
Whose little life is spent
In weaving from its tender form
Its precious monument,

He loved, who other life resigned
To live in what he wrought;
In the rich web wrapped up and shrined
Of his own matchless thought.

This tree, that from his own took birth,
Grows as that grew before; —
His buried genius left on earth
No like nor suc'cessor.

TO A LADY,

WHO COMPLAINED THAT HER HEART HAD LOST ITS YOUTH.

TIME withers up the fairest face,
Throws tower and palace down,
Steals from the noblest form its grace,
And rusts out sword and crown;
The tree is for its rotting sway,
The stone is for its tooth; —
But oh! take back that word, nor say
That hearts can lose their youth.

The heart is of no earthly mould,
Is neither clay nor rock;
Nor snaps like steel, nor dulls like gold,
Nor yields to wear or shock.
Its strength is in its loving will;
Its life is in its truth;
Then, lady, do not tell me still,
Your heart has lost its youth.

THE HEART'S DIALOGUE.

"There 's scarce an hour of any day
I could not drop to sleep;
There 's scarce an hour, I almost say,
I would not gladly weep.

" The laboring cares that strain the mind
Fall heavy on the eyes,
And griefs that never speak would find
Relief in more than sighs.

" This is not sluggishness that droops;
These are not passion's tears;
The spirit strives as well as stoops,
And praises while it fears.

" No; here 's the weary weight, — that all
So empty seems to be;
And these pent drops, if shed, would fall
For others, not for me."

" Rouse, rouse thy mind; and every power
To life's great service bring;
Cheer, cheer thee, heart! and every hour
Learn not to pine, but sing.

"Then o'er this emptiness of earth
Will God's own fulness stream,
And bathe in light of holiest birth
The sorrow and the dream.

"Let slumber be but gathering strength,
And tears but Nature's debt;
So trouble shall be peace at length,
With dews of glory wet."

AN EPITHALAMIUM.

NIGHT OF JULY 13, 1843.

To H. W. L.

Now is there light in earth and heaven,
From tapers and from stars.
The first bright sign on high is given
"To the red planet Mars."

And Saturn, falsely called of lead,
　　Shoots from the Archer's bow;
With mystic ring and moons, is shed,
　　All round, his golden glow.

And lo! another orb appears,
　　That makes those great ones least;
For Jove his locks ambrosial rears
　　From the religious East.

May each celestial influence blend
　　To bless this nuptial rite; —
E'en sunny Hermes backward send
　　His smile upon the night!

O brightest beam! though absent now
　　From that broad arch above,
Deck, morn and eve, this life-long vow,
　　Thou constant Star of Love!

TO THE SHADE OF ROBERT HERRICK.

Yes, all that 's bright and sweet and fair
    Soon finds its season past,
    And shrinks and withers fast;
And we who gaze on it the while
    But shine and bloom and smile,
        To cease at last.

Yet not for this let man despair.
    The lily ever lives
    That Innocency gives;
And though the glittering stars turn pale,
    No rays of Truth shall fail,
        And Hope survives.

A NATIONAL ODE.

SUNG ON THE 203D ANNIVERSARY OF THE ANCIENT AND HONORABLE ARTILLERY COMPANY, JUNE 7, 1841.

Tune, — *The Marseillaise.*

Sons of the free, be true to glory,
And be that glory true — and wise!
O heed your noble fathers' story!
O see the waiting nations' eyes!
That story fires the world already
With generous deeds for freedom done;
Those eyes pursue the westering sun,
To watch you with their gazes steady.
Stand close, ye chosen line,
And vindicate your birth!
March on! — your bannered stars shall shine
A blessing o'er the earth.

No spoil that 's won by fraud or plunder
E'er swell the treasures of your state!

No wars, with fratricidal thunder,
    Storm out your place among the great!
Let master-skill, and patient labor,
    And Heaven's own gifts, your store increase;
    And be the strength of honest Peace
For fiery shot and bloody sabre.
        Stand close, &c.

Ye late were few, that now are many;
    Ye late were weak, that now are strong;
Beyond the ridgy Alleghany,
    From sea to sea ye roll along.
O keep the brother-bond for ever,
    That knits your numbers into one!
    Be sure your praise is all undone,
Should jealous feuds that Union sever.
        Stand close, &c.

Let Knowledge wear her crown upon her!
    Your cry go forth: "More light! More light!"

And every spot that marks dishonor
    Fade off from all your scutcheons white!
Through burning suns and sleety weather,—
    Let weal or adverse fates befall,—
    Together hark to God's great call,
And rise and reign, or sink,—together.
        Stand close, &c.

Set high the throne of heavenly Order;
    Revere the shield and blade of Law;—
From central point to farthest border
    Beheld with love, obeyed with awe.
Unruly factions ne'er mislead you!
    Calm as the angel Michael stood,
    Keep at your feet hell's ruffian brood,
With right to arm, and God to speed you!
    Stand close, ye chosen line,
        And vindicate your birth!
March on!—your bannered stars shall shine
        A blessing o'er the earth.

DANIEL WEBSTER.

WRITTEN AT SUNSET, OCTOBER 22, 1852.

Sink, thou Autumnal Sun!
The trees will miss the radiance of thine eye,
Clad in their Joseph-coat of many a dye;
The clouds will miss thee in the fading sky;
But now in other scenes thy race must run,
This day of glory done.

Sink, thou of nobler light!
The land will mourn thee in its darkening hour;
Its heavens grow gray at thy retiring power,
Thou shining orb of mind, thou beacon-tower!
Be thy great memory still a guardian might,
When thou art gone from sight.

ODE

SUNG AT THE DORCHESTER CELEBRATION OF JULY 4, 1855.

OLD Dorchester has fame to wear,
  Won from the days of Faith and Strife ;—
The Faith that winged the Pilgrims' prayer,
  The War that breathed a Nation's life.

In front she stood, when first arose
  The church upon the red man's shore ;
In front, to meet the shock of foes,
  When opened Freedom's cannon-roar.

Her heights have felt the foot and eye
  Of him who led our victories on ;
Her plains run seaward, as to vie
  With some yet future Marathon.

Old Dorchester is glad to-day ;
  Her sacred bells ring feast and mirth;
Her gunners' trains and war-array
  But shoot their joy to sky and earth.

Old Dorchester is proud to-day!
  Through her own lips its trump is blown ;
And he,* who speaks what she would say,
  By twofold title is her own.

Old Hundred.

O God of Faith and Armies! Now
Make pure our thanks, lift high our vow.
Thy Spirit be thy people's might,
And valor guard their free birthright!

* Hon. Edward Everett.

TO AN INVALID.

THE rose is on thy cheek, sweet maid,
The lily on thy brow;
Though on thy form the hurt is laid,
That keeps it bowed so low.

There 's patience in those gentle eyes,
And courage in that smile ;
And active thoughts, not pining sighs,
Are in thy heart the while.

The learned page is at thy side,
The pencil in thy hand ;
While round thee shapes of beauty glide,
And truths of reverence stand.

Thy soul is with the sparkling spheres,
And with the flowery ground ;
And listens with attuned ears
To Nature's wealth of sound.

The voices of a various lore
Thy studious spirit teach ;
They come from many a distant shore,
In many a foreign speech.

But most to thee that blessed book
Of pentecostal flame ;
Kindling to tongues as still we look,
In every speech the same.

I love thee for thy cultured mind,
Thy temper firm and mild;
More for the ingenuous heart I find
Of honor undefiled.

Might I but aid thy languid strength,
And guide thy suffering way,
Till pain and weakness drop at length,
And shadows melt in day!

STRENGTH.

TO A FRIEND NEAR DEATH.

"When I am weak, I 'm strong,"
The great Apostle cried.
The strength, that did not to the earth belong,
The might of Heaven supplied.

"When I am weak, I 'm strong";—
Blind Milton caught that strain,
And flung its victory o'er the ills that throng
Round Age, and Want, and Pain.

"When I am weak, I 'm strong,"
Each Christian heart repeats;
These words will tune its feeblest breath to song,
And fire its languid beats.

"When I am weak, I 'm strong"; —
That saying is for you,
Dear friend, and well it may become your tongue,
Whose soul has found it true.

O Holy Strength! whose ground
Is in the heavenly land;
And whose supporting help alone is found
In God's immortal hand.

O blessed! that appears
When fleshly aids are spent;
And girds the mind, when most it faints and fears,
With trust and sweet content.

It bids us cast aside
All thoughts of lesser powers;
Give up all hopes from changing time and tide,
And all vain will of ours.

We have but to confess
That there 's but one retreat;
And meekly lay each need and each distress
Down at the Sovereign Feet;—

Then, then it fills the place
Of all we hoped to do;
And sunken Nature triumphs in the Grace
That bears us up and through.

A better glow than health
Flushes the cheek and brow;
The heart is stout with store of nameless wealth;—
We can do all things now.

No less sufficience seek;
All counsel less is wrong;
The whole world's force is poor, and mean, and weak; —
"When I am weak, I'm strong."

IN A FUNERAL ALBUM.

The parents' hearts in anguish bade farewell.
How well she fares, an angel's tongue shall tell,
Far from the reach of every funeral knell,
In that blest time rung in with heavenly bell,
In that blest land where beauteous spirits dwell.

A DEPARTURE.

"Weep not; she is not dead."

No! call it not to die, to pass away
Thus, and to be translated; — every power
Of mind and spirit kept till life's last breath;
No pain to rack the frame; no weak regret
Or anxious doubt to cloud the parting soul;
Peace in the heart, and hope upon the brow, —
Ay, more than hope, — faith changing into vision,
As this bright world, with all its bloom upon it,
Was opening upward into views of heaven.
This is not death, but ceasing to be mortal.
It may remind us of those old departures,
Those exoduses, told in Holy Writ,
Which that word "dead" was not allowed to
 darken.
"And Enoch walked with God; and he was not,
For God had taken him." — "And he was not," —

Not on the earth, where he had walked so long, —
As many years as each year shines in days, —
But lost to human eyesight; disappearing
Within the splendor where he walks for ever.

When Israel's prophet, he that was its chariot
And horsemen, felt that his last hour was come, —
His last below, — a fiery car and steeds
Of fire his fervid spirit snatched away.
It was not so with her. No troubled sky,
No shapes of terrible beauty, broke the calm,
That blest her sweet translation from the world.
O mourn not for her! Mourn but for the dead, —
The dead in sins, the dead in hopelessness.
She has but just put on her incorruption.

TO THE OLD FAMILY CLOCK,

SET UP IN A NEW PLACE.

Old things are come to honor. Well they might,
If old like thee, thou reverend monitor!
So gravely bright, so simply decorated,
Thy gold but faded into softer beauty,
While click and hammer-stroke are just the same
As when my cradle heard them. Thou hold'st on,
Unwearied, unremitting, constant ever;
The time that thou dost measure leaves no mark
Of age or sorrow on thy gleaming face;
The pulses of thy heart were never stronger;
And thy voice rings as clear as when it told me
How slowly crept the impatient days of childhood.
More than a hundred years of joys and troubles
Have passed and listened to thee, while thy tongue
Still told in its one round the unvaried tale;—

The same to thee, to them how different,
As fears, regrets, or wishes gave it tone!

My mother's childish wonder gazed as mine did
On the raised figures of thy slender door; —
The men — or dames — Chinese, grotesquely human;
The antlered stag beneath its small, round window;
The birds above, of scarce less size than he;
The doubtful house; the tree unknown to nature.

I see thee not in the old-fashioned room,
That first received thee from the mother-land;
But yet thou mind'st me of those ancient times
Of homely duties and of plain delights,
Whose love, and mirth, and sadness sat before thee,—
Their laugh and sigh both over now, their voices
Sunk and forgotten, and their forms but dust.

Thou, for their sake, stand honored *there* awhile, —
Honored wherever standing, — ne'er to leave
The house that calls me master. When there 's
none such,
I thus bequeath thee, as in trust, to those
Who shall bear up my name.
For each that hears
The music of thy bell, strike on the hours, —
Duties between, and Heaven's great hope beyond
them.

TO A DEAD TREE,

WITH A VINE TRAINED OVER IT.

The dead tree bears; each dried-up bough
With leaves is overgrown,
And wears a living drapery now
Of verdure not its own.

The worthless stock a use has found,
The unsightly branch a grace,
As, climbing first, then dropped around,
The green shoots interlace.

So round that Grecian mystic rod
To Hermes' hand assigned, —
The emblem of a helping god, —
First leaves, then serpents, twined.

In thee a holier sign I view
Than in Hebrew rods of power ;
Whether they to a serpent grew,
Or budded into flower.

This vine, but for thy mournful prop,
Would ne'er have learned the way
Thy ruined height to overtop,
And mantle thy decay.

O thou, my Soul, thus train thy thought
By Sorrow's barren aid!
Deck with the charms that Faith has brought
The blights that Time has made.

On all that is remediless
Still hang thy gentle veils;
And make thy charities a dress,
Where other foliage fails.

The sharp, bare points of mortal lot
With kindly growths o'erspread;—
Some blessing on what pleases not,
Some life on what is dead.

THE FOUR HALCYON POINTS OF THE YEAR.

Four points divide the skies,
Traced by the Augur's staff in days of old:
"The spongy South," — the hard North, gleaming cold, —
And where days set and rise.

Four seasons span the Year:
The flowering Spring, the Summer's ripening glow,
Autumn with sheaves, and Winter in its snow; —
Each brings its separate cheer.

Four Halcyon periods part
With gentle touch each season into twain,
Spreading o'er all in turn their gentle reign.
O mark them well, my heart!

Janus! the first is thine.
After the freezing Solstice locks the ground, —
When the keen blasts that moan or rave around
Show not one softening sign, —

It interposes then.
The air relents; the ices thaw to streams;
A mimic Spring shines down with hazy beams,
Ere Winter roars again.

Look thrice four weeks from this.
The vernal days are rough in our stern clime;
Yet fickle April wins a mellow time,
Which chilly May shall miss.

Another term is run.
She comes again, the peaceful one, though less
Or needed or perceived in Summer dress, —
Half lost in the bright Sun.

Yet then a place she finds,
And all beneath the sultry calm lies hush, —
Till o'er the chafed and darkening Ocean rush
The squally August winds.

Behold her yet once more,
And O how beautiful! Late in the wane
Of the dishevelled Year, when hill and plain
Have yielded all their store, —

When the leaves, thin and pale,
And they not many, tremble on the bough,
Or, noisy in their crisp decay, e'en now
Roll to the sharpening gale, —

In smoky lustre clad,
Its warm breath flowing in a parting hymn,
The "Indian Summer" upon Winter's rim
Looks on us sweetly sad.

So with the year of Life.
An Ordering Goodness helps its youth and age,
Posts quiet sentries midway every stage,
And gives it truce in strife.

The Heavenly Providence,
With varying methods but a steady hold,
Doth trials still with mercies interfold,
For human soul and sense.

The Father that 's above
Remits, assuages; still abating one
Of all the stripes due to the ill that 's done,
In his compassionate love.

Help Thou our wayward mind
To own Thee constantly in all our states, —
The world of Nature and the world of Fates, —
Forbearing, tempering, kind.

THE McLEAN ASYLUM, SOMERVILLE.

O House of Sorrows! How thy domes
Swell on the sight, but crowd the heart;
While pensive Fancy walks thy rooms,
And shrinking Memory minds me what thou art!

A rich, gay mansion once wert thou;
And he who built it chose its site
On that hill's proud, but gentle brow,
For an abode of splendor and delight.

Years, pains, and cost have reared it high,
The stately pile we now survey,
Grander than ever to the eye; —
But all its fireside pleasures, — where are they?

A stranger might suppose the spot
  Some seat of learning, shrine of thought; —
Ah! here alone Mind ripens not,
And nothing reasons, nothing can be taught.

Or he might deem thee a retreat
  For the poor body's need and ail;
When sudden injuries stab and beat,
Or in slow waste its inward forces fail.

Ah, heavier hurts and wastes are here!
  The ruling brain distempered lies.
When Mind flies reeling from its sphere,
Life, health, ay, mirth itself, are mockeries.

O House of Sorrows! sorest shocks
  That can our frame or lot befall
Are hid behind thy jealous locks;
Man's Thought an infant, and his Will a thrall.

The mental, moral, bodily parts,
So nicely separate, strangely blent,
Fly on each other in mad starts,
Or sink together, wildered all and spent.

The sick — but with fantastic dreams!
The sick — but from their uncontrol!
Poor, poor humanity! What themes
Of grief and wonder for the musing soul!

Friends have I seen from free, bright life
Into thy dull confinement cast;
And some, through many a weeping strife,
Brought to that last resort, — the last, the last.

O House of Mercy! Refuge kind
For nature's most unnatural state!
Place for the absent, wandering mind!
Its healing helper and its sheltering gate!

What woes did man's own cruel fear
Once add to his crazed brother's doom!
Neglect, aversion, tones severe,
The chain, the lash, the fetid, living tomb.

And now behold what different hands
He lays on that crazed brother's head.
See how this builded bounty stands,
With scenes of beauty all around it spread.

Yes, Love has planned thee, Love endowed.
And blessings on each pitying heart,
That from the first its gifts bestowed,
Or bears in thee each day its patient part!

Was e'er the Christ diviner seen,
Than when the wretch no force could bind,
The roving, raving Gadarene,
Sat at his blessed feet, and in his perfect mind?

TO ELSIE.

I.

NOTHING was there, save one fair tree,
In Summer's glory drest ;
I plucked a leaf, for thought of thee,
And hid it in my breast.

And now its mates are changed and gone,
Nipped by the Autumn's chill,
Drooping and dropping one by one, —
But this is verdant still ;

And will remain, in hue and form,
As I behold it now,
Let sultry gale or freezing storm
Disturb the parent bough.

So when the blooming charms depart,
Which Joy's brief season gives,
Unchanging, in the silent heart,
A severed memory lives.

II.

A MALADY too dread to name
In one I've held so dear!
The sharp thrills shooting through thy frame
Are deadly darts, we fear.

Yet do not think thy suffering state
Too different from our own ;
The dark seeds of a certain fate
In all our flesh are sown.

Of any two, who dares to say
Which shall the first be gone ?

If best, years distant or to-day,
Who knows of any *one* ?

Then cease to guess of times, dear friend,
Or how their lot may fall ;
One gracious Hand ordains the end
So doubtful for us all.

Live in that dateless, deathless part,
Which keeps its health and youth ;
The Eternal in man's loving heart,
And in God's holy truth.

III.

DEAD, dead and gone !
Thou too hast joined the train
Of those I ne'er shall see again ; —
The world is growing lone.

They fall how fast!
Mates of my fresher prime,
Associates of my waning time,
The passing and the past.

O "tale that 's told"!
How many feebly stay!
How many went but yesterday!
What griefs already old!

New sorrow now!
Fair friend, through many a year
Of spirits light and feelings dear,
Thou must desert me, — thou!

And not one word
To mark the closing Scene,
After such meetings as have been?
Speak, — or let me be heard.

Come back! Once more
Thy slender hand be set
In mine. One prayer together yet
We 'll breathe, ere all is o'er.

Meek shade, forgive!
I would not have thee back,
Stretched out again on this world's rack.
Go forth, go forth, to live.

A MEDITATION.

Too far from thee, O Lord!
The world is close upon each captured sense;
The heart's dear idols never vanish hence;
Life's care and labor still are pressing nigh;

Its fates and passions hard about me lie ; —
But Thou art dim behind thine infinite sky,
O distantly adored !

O Lord, too far from thee !
Unwingèd Time stands ever in my sight,
Flooding the Past and Now with gloom and light ;
Silent, but busy, constant at my side,
It shreds away strength, beauty, joy, and pride.
Eternal ! why am I from Thee so wide,
Nor thy near Presence see ?

Ne'er languished for as now.
Now that the hold of Earth feels poor and frail, —
Now that the cheek of Hope looks thin and pale,
And forms of buried love rise ghostly round,
And dark thoughts struggle on o'er broken ground, —
Where is thy face, O Father ! radiant found
With mercy on the brow ?

I know that not from far,
Not from abroad, this presence is revealed, —
To our will denied, and from our wit concealed.
No search can find Thee, no entreaty bring, —
Reason a weak, Desert a spotted thing.
O Spirit, lift me on thy dove-like wing
To realms that last and ARE!

—⬦—

THE AUTUMNAL EQUINOX.

ROOM for King Autumn! Room!
Summer, the wanton queen, has run to doom,
And died. With warlike din,
The rude but bounteous conqueror marches in.
See how his banners fly,
The gonfalons of cloud and stain-streaked sky.
Hark to his pipe and drum!
On the fierce blast their stormy clangors come; —

They whistle and they beat
O'er the wide ocean, through the narrow street;
While to their terrible call
The surges mount, and tree and turret fall.
His cannon on the air
Flashes and roars. It is his sign! Room there!

Now he is sitting crowned;
And golden sunsets beam his brows around,
And ruddy noontide hours
Warm up the thin leaves of his mottled bowers.
At night the moon's pale face
Rises before its time, to do him grace.
Now plenteous fruits — not such
As those before them, mouldering soon from touch,
But hardy, ripening still
For use long hence — the patient garners fill.

O equinoctial time,
Whose days are southing towards the frosty clime

Of this strange life! In raids
Of storm and wrath at first thy power invades;
And at the ominous gale
Which Nature shakes at, a poor heart may quail.
New King, be good to me!
Let me thy mellow favors round me see,
And something laid in store,
When leaves have dropped and flowers will bloom
no more.
And take not clean away
The genial glows that warmed a longer day.
Hunters' and Harvest moon,
Loath to desert, and coming up so soon,
Be emblems to my mind
Of love, that when most needed shows most kind;
And all that crimson West
Breathe of pavilioned hopes and no ignoble rest.

ODYSSEUS AND CALYPSO.

Now blest be the lightning that shivered thy bark,
Strong swimmer through surges and destinies dark!
Here, free from all woes, — toil and sea-storm and
fight, —
This isle of the blest yields thee peace and delight.
Not a lovelier land do the ocean streams lave,
With the lip of its shore to the breast of the wave.
Isle of fragrance and fruitage, of fountain and grot,
Where the strifes you've escaped from may all be
forgot;
Where ambrosia the food, and pure nectar the
bowl,
Are the least of the dainties that ravish the soul.
What the songs of its sky, and the blooms of its
scene,

To the graces of Nymphs with a Goddess for queen,
When her beauty divine does not shun to impart
Every charm for the senses, and heart for thy heart,
Breathing round thee that joy every rapture above,—
That heaven of the spirit, — the magic of love?
And more — O how much! — she will raise thee to be
The peer of her nature, immortal as she;
No creeping of age o'er thy limbs or thy brow,
But for ever as strong and as ardent as now.
Odysseus the wanderer, repose thee at last!
Odysseus the mortal, here fix thy life fast!
Odysseus, thou schemer! here 's more to thy hand
Than a man ever reached, than thy thought ever spanned.
O chief much-enduring! thy labors now stay;
And Odysseus the wise! show thou art so to-day.

Such once my thoughts, when through the pictured page
Of the great poet-fabulist my eye
Followed the fates of heroes; — chiefly his
Whose mythic story fills the Odyssey.
Short-sighted judgment! He the Ithacan,
So crowned by Nature and so tossed by Fortune,
Assisted and pursued by Powers Divine,
Inventive, bold, loving, and eloquent,
The child of tears and fire, set forth to war
With chances various as his moods and gifts,
Is but the emblem of the spirit and lot
Revealed within our frail humanity.
Stand forth, ye shapes of Memory and of Faith,
And show how humanly Odysseus chose; —
Scorning to be immortal; ease and pleasure
Storming aside; and, passion against passion,
Leaving a Goddess, but to grow "divine."
I listen for your voices.

THE SPIRIT OF CURIOSITY:

"O who can bear a changeless state?
Joy is not joy, however great,
That travels still its former round,
And seeks but what 's already found.
What boots it to repeat—repeat—
What cloys the more, so rich and sweet?
Harped to one note, what ear or brain
But aches with the unvaried strain?
The New, the Further, stirs the thought;
And all before or seen or taught,
With naught to come, itself is naught.
Who would for ages tamely lie
In ignorance and monotony?
What! shall this islet's narrow close
Bound all that sage Odysseus knows,
And one sequestered, shady nook
Veil the whole world from his keen look?
Rouse, rouse thy well-experienced mind,
Longer to seek and more to find."

THE SPIRIT OF ACTION:

"O noble son of Laertes, the versatile, wily Odysseus!
Warrior of many fields, and lord of a thousand devices,
Outreaching Circe, fair witch, and the cannibal giant, the Round-Eye!
Where now those charms of speech, that bowed whole armies to hear thee?
Where thy rank in the council-hall, thy praise in the roll of achievement,
The stealthy delight of the ambush, the rapturous rage of the onset,
And all the stirring of heart that gladdens a prince and a leader?
What is more wearying to man than sloth and a passive indulgence?
The life of his life is pursuit, and the cheer of successes;

And even the gods themselves can crown but desert and endeavor.
Remember thy bow where it hangs, and that only thy sinews can bend it;
Remember, that purpose and deed and spirit alone are enduring.
Once more o'er the wine-dark sea, to thyself and thy work and thy glory."

THE SPIRIT OF CONSCIENCE:

" In vain we seek for rest
In couch and sports and cheer;
There cries a voice within the breast:
'Art thou obedient here?'

"The Duty that we owe,
Yet fear or hate to meet,
Will dash with gall and secret woe
The draught we deem most sweet.

" The Duty we perform,
Though hard, if bravely done,
Will pour a light through thickest storm
More blessed than the sun.

" Revere the soul within;
Revere the gods on high;
Nor dream a precious prize to win
By a disloyalty.

" Odysseus! foremost name
In Grecian tale and song;
Can you retreat from all that fame,
To sluggishness and wrong?

" What guard is for thy hall?
What counsel for thy child?
And who will keep thy subjects all
From foes and factions wild?

"Shame, — thus in ease to bask,
And wanton, and depend!
Up! to achieve a true man's task,
And reach a true man's end."

THE SPIRIT OF LONGING.

On the lone shore Odysseus sits, — his eyes,
Strained on the wide sea and the wider skies,
Filling with tears; — his own land that way lies.
The years long past, before the sail for Troy,
Roll o'er his heart, and bury all its joy;
His first ambitions and his pastimes young, —
His dogs and boar-spear the wild rocks among, —
His friends so many on that natal shore,
Some looking for him back, some seen themselves no more, —
His sire, if age and trouble spare him yet, —
These rise around, in vivid pictures set;
Yet fade before the thoughts, that thronging come,

Of his true wedded one at home, at home;
And of the princely boy to manhood grown,
Heir of his father's fame, to win his own.
Then the home-longing pang distracts his heart,
And from his lips these words impatient start: —

"The bright sky is pale,
And the pure air is thick,
And my strong powers fail
As they grow fancy-sick.

"My brain madly floats
Between yearning and fear,
And saddens and dotes; —
I 'm a prisoner here.

"This rest is no ease;
These delights are but pain
Again for the seas!
For my hearthstone again!

" The pleasures are lone
These immortals supply; —
Away for MY OWN,
And behold them or die!"

TRIFLINGS.

SONG,

SUNG AT THE OPENING OF THE "TREMONT HOUSE," OCTOBER 16, 1829.

Air, — "*The Moon 's on the Lake.*"

GOOD cheer has a good special blessing upon 't ;—
Then hail to you, House of the Stranger, TRE-
MONT !
Your proud, ample walls hearty welcome bespeak
In the plain English tongue, though your porch is
all Greek.
Then halloo! halloo! halloo !
Its stones and its bread we have piled up for
others,

To the ends of the land our compatriots and
brothers.
Then gather, gather, gather, gather, gather,
gather!
Till our granite flows down like the tide of a river,
Our Fathers' "TREA-MOUNTAIN" shall flourish for
ever.

Come, come, from the lands of the warm, sunny
South,
From the Cumberland's foot and the Edisto's
mouth!
Come, come, from the prairies and streams of the
West!
For the worst that we give is enough of the best.
Then halloo! halloo! halloo!
There is room for us all 'neath our Eagle's broad
pinion;
Young Maine may pledge healths with "the Ancient Dominion."

Then gather, gather, gather, &c.
Till our granite flows down like the tide of a river,
Our Fathers' "Trea-mountain" shall flourish for
ever.

Come on, from the peak of our easternmost
rock, —
Androscoggin, and Schoodic, and Sagadahoc!
Come on, from the North where the Winter "burns
frore,"
From Memphremagog's ice and Niagara's roar!
Then halloo! halloo! halloo!
Let the mountains bow round, from the "White"
to the "Rocky,"
And Missouri kiss waves with sweet Winnipi-
seogee.
Then gather, gather, gather, &c.
Till our granite flows down like the tide of a river,
Our Fathers' "Trea-mountain" shall flourish for
ever.

LINES

ON THE RESTORATION OF THE FEDERAL STREET THEATRE.

The FEDERAL STREET THEATRE, after having been put to several uses, was restored to the purpose for which it was originally built, and resumed its performances on the evening of August 27, 1846. The following lines were written, as if for the Address on that occasion; though not offered for recitation or prize.

O'ER life's quick scenes not many years have flown,
Since wondering nations hailed "THE GREAT UNKNOWN."
A world's fond wishes could not keep him long,
That king of fiction and that child of song;
He shrunk to dust who swayed our hearts at will,
And Dryburgh's Ruin shrined a nobler still.

But leave that broken spell and its lost lord; —
Look round to-night; — here see THE GREAT RESTORED; —
Restored to that old form we held so dear,
To healthful laugh and purifying tear,
To scenic art, the Drama's acted page,
And all the guiltless witchcraft of the Stage, —
Restored to many a Memory's crowding host, —
Restored to every Muse it sadly lost.
Hail, the returning Spirit of the place,
Banished so long! Hail, each recovered grace!
Hail, renewed spot! In thee the oldest here
Call back the figures of life's magic year,
When all seemed real in this mimic show,
And all beamed wondrous in young Fancy's glow;
When ear and sight with strange delights were fed,
As these scant boards to spacious regions spread;
When men looked giants by the painted trees,*

* This illusion was very strong upon my boyish eyes, at their first sight of a play. The persons who stood at the side of the stage

And Mirth and Terror strove which most could
please.
How the heart fluttered at the prompter's bell!
What visions faded when the curtain fell!
Not all the forms the "Wizard of the North"
In light and beauty ever summoned forth
So live and move before the thought, as those
That spoke embodied as that curtain rose.
These rounding seats a whole charmed circle grew;
That line of foot-lights bounded worlds all new.

But think what changes here have held their sway,
Since all those tricksy Powers were forced away.
Scarce were they banished, when a rabble throng
Of scoffing spirits gloomed these walls along.

---

in a garden-scene appeared colossal, but diminished as they approached the centre of the boards. This optical marvel was never perfectly repeated, being unconsciously corrected by observation. The philosophical solution of it, however, was not suggested till long afterwards.

Not fallen from Heaven,— for they were never
there;—
Their law low pleasure, and their creed despair.*
No graceful ticket gave the entrance then;—
'T was "largest liberty's" most noisome den.
No "Hats off!" rang the sullen ranks between;—
What was respected? What was to be seen?
The audience dingy, far as eye could reach,—
A gray-haired atheist spectacle and speech.
Was it for this, ye foemen of our art,
Who think there 's but one way to touch the heart,
And that your own,— was it for this ye beat
The genial Sisters from their ancient seat,
Turning this intellectual, brilliant dome
To stupid Blasphemy's disordered home?
Was this your "Players' Lash," ye modern
Prynnes,†—

* The deserted Theatre fell first into the hands of Abner Kneeland and his followers.

† Poor William Prynne's "Histrio-Mastix" was published in 1632.

To scourge enjoyments, while you beckoned sins?
Was this your preference 'twixt the Outs and Ins?

But lo! another change, like Stockwell's own!
The DEN has vanished, and a CHURCH is shown.*
More reverence than befits us here to tell,
We yield to courts where sacred honors dwell.
But have not they their places? Have not we?
Has not each liberal province leave to be?
Not every building for one use is raised,
Nor any use is singly to be praised.
All School, Inn, Hospital, were dull indeed;
Our honest Playhouse but for life would plead.

But whence the name ODEON? Here we track
Another change, in these our fortunes, back.
O Music, charming though no word be sung!

* The religious society here gathered built afterwards the "Central Church" in Winter Street, under the pastoral care of the lamented William M. Rogers.

What stringed expression! What an air-shaped
tongue!
Far be from us the jealous heart, to slight
The listening transport of each tuneful night!
And yet the ACADEMY's most skilful powers
In scope and number surely yield to ours.
Here all the Aonian maids their gifts combine;—
And who will say that One was worth the Nine?

Another metamorphosis recall
To Memory ranging round this scenic hall.
As if the last Muse left had met her doom,—
Euterpe gone,—behold a LECTURE-ROOM.
A sober uniformity bears rule,
While old and wise here gravely come to school.
Now, deepest Learning highest truths imparts;
Now Genius, Eloquence, entrance all hearts.
But where the various splendor that here blazed?
The various interest that here breathless gazed?
The stage was but a chair; the scene became
An illustration, or a diagram.

The whole machinery presented then
A planetarium, or a *specimen.*
No fictions clad in colored glories shone,
But all was real as a fossil bone.
Star-eyed Urania spoke in broadcloth suit;
Unlaurelled Clio walked without her lute.
Solid Philosophies their facts display,
As sixty patient minutes grant delay ;
Or mystic thought ideal pictures draws,
While transcendental bonnets nod applause.

Enough of this. We own, as own we must,
These walls were honored by a use so just;
And, while they stand to win new rights to fame,
Rejoice to have been allied to LOWELL'S name.*

Restored! Restored! Well known so long a time,
These buried glories rise as in their prime.

---

* The celebrated LOWELL LECTURES were inaugurated here, December 31, 1839, with an Address by Hon. Edward Everett.

Our tastes may change, as fickle fashions fly,
But Art is safe; the Drama cannot die.
More than restored! Whate'er the pen since wrought
Of loftiest, sprightliest, here that wealth has brought.
Whate'er the progress of the age has lent
Of purer taste and comelier ornament, —
To this our temple it transfers its store,
And makes each point shine lovelier than before.

But more yet, — and how much! We claim a praise
The Playhouse knew not in the ancient days.
Own us, ye hearts with moral purpose warm!
Our word Renewal adds the word Reform.
Too long the Drama's garments have been stained
By vices not her own. Accused, arraigned,
Condemned, she hopeless stood. Her fate has been
To allow, and suffer for, a foreign sin.

Not all unjust. For foul abuses cleaved
Fast to her skirts; though never unperceived,
Never washed out; — and thus a blame she bears
Which nothing in her nature needs or shares.
We have effaced this blot; nor more endure
In Gallery or Saloon the vicious lure.
No cups of sparkling ruin gleam below;
No frail disgraces fill an upper row.
All bad alliances we safely spurn,
And scorn the favor we must basely earn.
To purest service of our Art we now
Its long-dismantled Temple freshly vow,
And to its cause the proudest works devote,
That ever Taste contrived or Genius wrote.
Come each, and help us! Be our Drama's friend!
Some it instructs, and none it need offend.
Hearts are improved by Feeling's play and strife;
Refined amusement humanizes life.
So wrote the Sages, whom the world admired;
So sang the Poets, who the world inspired;

Why in New England's Athens is decried
What old Athenian culture thought its pride?

Again we bid our Thespian ensigns fly;
Teach through the emotions, lecture to the eye;
Again to Nature hold the mirror up;
Again our emblems, — dagger, mask, and cup!
Act we, and not recite, that bard sublime,
Who "was not of an age, but for all time."
Come, friends of Virtue! Share the feast we spread.
It loads no spirits, and it heats no head;
But rouses forth each power of mind and soul
With food ambrosial and its fairy bowl.
Your "masters of the revels" we appear,
And greet you. Give us back one hearty cheer.
The Roman actors, when the play was done,
Cried out, Applaud! Then first their prize was won.
Reward our greater boldness, friends! for we
Make our commencement with our "Plaudite!"

A WINTER SOLILOQUY.

WILL Summer ever come again?
Will Winter ever pass?
Shall we have for frost the soft, warm rain,
And for ice the fresh, green grass?

Will the trees put on their glossy gear?
Will the birds take up their song,
And new-born shapes of life and cheer
Glance merrily along?

Shall I bare my brow for the air's cool wreath?
Shall I see the dust whirled round?
And inhale, for my nostril's frozen breath,
The scents of the fragrant ground?

Shall I see again the sky's blue cope,
With bright clouds floating in 't?
And oh! shall I see a window ope,
Excepting in a print?

Shall we walk again "in silk attire,"
Nor fear for slipping down;
And, instead of the snow's cold glare, admire
The gleam of a snow-white gown?

Will cloaks drop off from shoulders fair,
And hoods from faces blue,
And delicate feet disdain to wear
The India-rubber shoe?

Shall boots and moccasons give place,
And muffling monsters all,
And Beauty show in the street its grace,
As in private bower and hall?

Yes! I hear the March-like winds arise;
The Spring will soon be here,
And birds, and flowers, and painted skies
Make glad the warming year.

But here my prophet gifts forsake,
Nor Fashion's freaks explore.
The cloak may still no difference make
'T wixt Fourteen and Fourscore;—

The belle may show her trousers still,
And boots may ne'er lay by,
And drag her unpronounceable
Caou — Caoutchoucs in July.

February 14, 1832.

XENIA.

THIS Greek word has found its way into the English Dictionary. It meant originally the presents that were made by a host to his departing guests; but afterwards, through various transitive meanings, came to denote gifts in general. Epigrammatic inscriptions for articles thus bestowed form a department, though a very humble one, of Latin literature. The word has been adopted by the French and Germans; the former using it most in the sense of new-year's gifts.

WITH A MOSAIC BUTTERFLY.

DISJOINTED, party-colored things
Here meet to form one whole,
And lo! an emblem spreads its wings; —
'T is Psyche! 'T is the Soul!

So time and life, O sister mine!
A checkered ground inlay ;
But wait till all the tints combine ; —
'T is Form, 't is Hope, 't is Day.

WITH A MOSAIC TABLE.

A TABLE here from Italy ; — the land
Which, though a foreign one, by you untrod,
You love to think of, and I often see
In well-remembered beauty rising clear.
No present seems more fit for you ; so pure
Its solid substance, — marble to the foot, —
Graceful but fixed, in sculptured symmetry.
Its firm-set base and its consistent stem
Seem like the strong and beautiful principles

That bear you up and yet are parts of you;
While the rich crowd of many-colored stones,
Harmonious though unlike, remind my heart
Of all the various treasures that inlay
The polished round of woman's excellence.

WITH A WATCH.

This cunning instrument has power
To trace the march of every hour,
And tell it to the eye.
It counts the minutes in their flow,
As, gliding swift or loitering slow,
They one by one pass by.

Its name, a Watch, denotes the care
Its use demands of those who wear;
It must not fall, nor stop.

Much more it warns us, not a day
Should fly in giddiness away,
Or into voidness drop.

A gift, then, with a meaning, here
Begins with you another year; —
This blessing with it take:
Beyond all dates and wastes of Time,
May goodness keep you in your prime,
And in your life's most wintry clime
A vernal beauty make!

WITH A FLOWERED FAN,

WHICH SPEAKS:

A SIMPLE gift for homely wear,
By your wearing, grace ;
And softest breath of sweetest air
Ever fan your face !

The sunny skies that warmly glow
Ask my fluttering aid ;
While brightest flowers around you blow,
Blooming but to fade.

The skies will back to chillness creep,
Summer signs be past;
But my sign its warmth will keep, —
My poor flowers will last.

WITH A PAIR OF SPECTACLES.

The glass set in gold
May soon break from its hold,
But the gold no such accident fears;
And so our frail senses
Are like these brittle lenses,
But the heart keeps the same all the years.

WITH A GOLD PEN IN IVORY.

In Solomon's throne,
They tell us, shone
" The ivory and the gold."
But all that pomp and pride
No solid use supplied.

Ere he who sat there died,
" All 's vanity," he cried ; —
They, like himself, were bought and sold.

These substances —
The same as his,
Though cast in such small mould —
Are here not set for show,
But faithful service owe ;
And almost seem to know
What help they will bestow
In telling what were else untold.

And so, dear, when
This strong, pure pen
Your fingers shall infold,
May words, like pure and strong,
Pour from its point along,
A free and blithesome throng, —
No thought or word writ wrong, —
And friends with friends glad converse hold.

WITH A COPY OF "VANITY FAIR."

Here is "Vanity Fair";
And well may you stare
At a title so strange and so new,
In whose heart lurks no vanity
Or pretending inanity,
And the selfish and false never grew.
Does not famed Mr. Thackeray
Of the best wisdom lack a ray,
When he writes down the world as untrue;
And to women above all
Pays but cynic approval, —
All silly, or vicious, or blue?
With his "insight" an outer,
And his spirit a flouter,
And a sinister twist in his view, —

Ah! he would not have painted
Folks so hollow and tainted,
Had he once been acquainted
With YOU.

WITH AN OPERA-GLASS.

An Opera-Glass
May seem hardly to pass,
Since so seldom you go
To a great public show.
But when you retreat
To your nice country-seat,
It may still find its uses,
If your ladyship chooses.

Sitting on your piazza,
You will find that it has a
Fine gift, to bring nigh
What would else miss your eye.
Distant houses and trees
Will come close as you please,
And the faint line of road
Will show clear and grow broad.

Nay, much farther yet
It will help you to get,
And not even at night
Give its power up quite.
The moon's edge and face
More plain it will trace ;
The disk of a planet, —
Why, you almost might span it;
And e'en the fixed star
Seems a little less far.

Take this for its say,
On this New Year's Day:
"Let all objects agreeable
Grow large and more seeable.
View those that offend
Through my opposite end;
That, if looked at at all,
They may look — very small."

So surveyed be Life's whole
Through the tubes of the soul!

WITH A MOSAIC "FORGET ME NOT."

ACCEPT and wear this constant flower,
    Thus copied out by art.
It blooms in Nature but its hour, —
    For ever in the heart.

Affections into habits grown, —
    Lives fastened in one lot, —
The flower has strengthened into stone
    We name "Forget me not."

WITH A BIBLE, ON A WEDDING-DAY.

A BETTER love than mine
This Holy Volume gives ;
It shows no shadow of decline,
And when I die it lives.

A love that 's constant still
To teach and cheer you through ;
That never frowns, " I may not will,"
Nor sighs, " I cannot do."

This Book binds man and wife
In closer loves and fears ;
And all the ties that bless our life
It hallows and endears.

Its blessing rest to-day
Upon your plighted troth ;
A blessing that shall always stay,
And grow upon you both!

TO H. E. S.

IN RETURN FOR A NACRE LETTER-FOLDER, AND SOME BEAUTIFUL LINES OF REMEMBRANCE.

WITH rainbowed pearl and sun-like phrase
You call to mind the past;—
Such tokens o'er the present days
A humid lustre cast.

THE END.

CORRECTION.

THE second line of Schiller's "Festival of Eleusis" should read the same as in the repeat at the end of the poem. The flower alluded to is called the Corn-Flower probably on account of its frequent growth among the wheat.

www.ingramcontent.com/pod-product-compliance
Lightning Source LLC
LaVergne TN
LVHW010131110826
845151LV00002B/327

* 9 7 8 1 4 2 5 5 3 9 8 8 7 *